MACMILLAN HISTORY OF LITERATURE

General Editor : A. NORMAN JEFFARES

MACMILLAN HISTORY OF LITERATURE

SIXTEENTH-CENTURY ENGLISH LITERATURE

Murray Roston

M

First published 1982 by
THE MACMILLAN PRESS LTD
Companies and representatives
throughout the world

ISBN 0 333 27143 2 (hc)
ISBN 0 333 27144 0 (pbk)

Typeset by
CAMBRIAN TYPESETTERS
Farnborough, Hants
Printed in Hong Kong

Contents

List of Plates

Acknowledgements

The author and publisher wish to acknowledge, with thanks, the following illustration sources:

By kind permission of his grace the Duke of Bedford, The Woburn Abbey Collection 12; The Bodleian Library 8, 9; The British Tourist Authority and by permission of the Marquis of Salisbury 10; The Folger Library, Washington/John Cranford Adams 13, 14; The Frick Collection 5; The Mansell Collection 2, 7; The National Gallery 6; The Newberry Library 3; The Royal Library, Windsor — by gracious permission of H.M. The Queen 4; Master & Fellows of St John's College, Cambridge 1; The Victoria and Albert Museum 11.

Editor's Preface

THE study of literature requires knowledge of contexts as well as texts. What kind of person wrote the poem, the play, the novel, the essay? What forces acted upon them as they wrote? What was the historical, the political, the philosophical, the economic, the cultural background? Was the writer accepting or rejecting the literary conventions of the time, or developing them, or creating entirely new kinds of literary expression? Are there interactions between literature and the art, music or architecture of its period? Was the writer affected by contemporaries or isolated?

Such questions stress the need for students to go beyond the reading of set texts, to extend their knowledge by developing a sense of chronology, of action and reaction, and of the varying relationships between writers and society.

Histories of literature can encourage students to make comparisons, can aid in understanding the purposes of individual authors and in assessing the totality of their achievements. Their development can be better understood and appreciated with some knowledge of the background of their time. And histories of literature, apart from their valuable function as reference books, can demonstrate the great wealth of writing in English that is there to be enjoyed. They can guide the reader who wishes to explore it more fully and to gain in the process deeper insights into the rich diversity not only of literature but of human life itself.

A. NORMAN JEFFARES

The dual vision

IN the earlier part of the sixteenth century, English literature certainly has its finer moments — the urbane prose of Sir Thomas More, the sonnets of Wyatt and Surrey, and the boisterous comedy of *Gammer Gurton's Needle*. Yet nothing within that century can match the surge of creativity which was so brilliantly to mark its final decades. In the brief space of some ten to fifteen years, what had been until then an essentially imitative literature looking towards the continent for its models came suddenly into its own, and the poetry of Sidney and Spenser, Marlowe and Shakespeare not only projected England to the forefront of the European scene, but set new standards against which the drama and poetry of future generations would be judged.

Modern scholarship now views with some scepticism the two traditional explanations for that phenomenon. The theory that it arose from England's national self-confidence as a growing economic and military power under the settled monarchy of Queen Elizabeth is less securely based than might at first appear. The country had indeed undergone profound changes during the century. The dissolution of the monasteries as Henry VIII broke away from Rome had transferred no less than one sixth of all cultivable land from the inefficient control of the monks to private hands, where it began to be worked intensively. The cloth trade boomed, coal-mining was developed, and cannon foundries were established to free the country from dependence on importation from abroad. By 1585 England had taken over the European lead in finance from Antwerp and become the centre for foreign investment. Elizabeth and her faithful advisor William Cecil, with the aid of the astute financier Sir Thomas Gresham, brought England from near bankruptcy in the mid-century to economic prosperity within the course of thirty years, till it rivalled the dominant power, Spain. War became inevitable, and the defeat of the Spanish Armada in 1588, when England's swift-sailing vessels outclassed the cumbersome and heavily manned Spanish vessels, changed naval strategy and left England with sufficient mastery of the seas to expand and develop its own independent trade routes.

'Economic prosperity', however, is an umbrella term that can cover a multitude of less attractive features. The rich had indeed become far richer, and the middle class was now established as a growing power in the land; but the poor, who still constituted the large majority in the country, had become miserably poorer. Food prices soared fivefold during the century with only a small rise in the average wage. The enclosure of land deprived many peasants of their livelihood, and rents were raised cruelly to cover the lavish expenses of the nobility. Accordingly, vagrancy and pillaging, the last resort of the desperate, became a major problem, which neither whipping nor repeated attempts at poor relief could stem. London teemed with beggars, whores, and cutpurses, the dross thrown up by waves of unemployment, and throughout Elizabeth's reign the tensions created by a discontented populace threatened to erupt into open rebellion. In brief, the economic boom of this period was often seen by the contemporaries who experienced it as a catastrophe rather than a blessing, in which, as Nashe put it, '. . . the usurer eateth up the gentleman, and the gentleman the yeoman, and all three, being devoured one of another, do nothing but complain.'[1] Lastly, in considering such new national wealth as the possible source of the literary revival, it should be remembered that writers in that period generally benefited least from it, the overwhelming majority struggling desperately against financial privation.

Even apart from that deeper disturbance in the country, the question remains whether national self-confidence based upon growing economic and military prowess is itself a prescription for producing great literature. The very reverse has often been proved true. Russian society was decaying and the Czarist regime on the way to its demise when Tolstoy, Dostoevsky, and Chekov produced their finest work; and in the 1930s Nazi Germany possessed to a remarkable degree both those qualities of military might and abounding national confidence and yet produced no literature of lasting significance. Even within the period we are now examining the indications are against that theory. Shakespeare's maturer plays, such as *King Lear*, *Othello*, and *Macbeth*, were written not during Elizabeth's reign but in the gloomier period of unrest at all levels of society under James I, and that fact suggests that it was, if anything, the insecurity of his time rather than the confidence which deepened his literary sensitivity.

The second theory placed the sudden burgeoning of English poetry and drama within the broader European setting as England's response to the continental revival of classical learning. The new interest in ancient authors which Petrarch and Boccaccio had helped to foster in fourteenth-century Italy received an added boost when a number of Greek scholars found their way westward at the fall of Constantinople to the Turks in 1453. With growing enthusiasm, libraries were searched for forgotten manuscripts, and scribes hired to copy them out for inclusion in private collections. Plato became a model for philosophical speculation, Cicero for prose 'eloquence', Ovid's *Metamorphoses* a source-book for mythology; and academies were established for the study of the ancient classics. This continental reverence for the past began to reach England in the early sixteenth century when Greek was included as a subject to be taught at the universities under William Grocyn and John Colet, with the encouragement of the famed Erasmus who was visiting England at that time. By mid-century the new grammar schools, such as Merchant Taylors, which had now been either founded or re-established to replace those previously conducted under monastic supervision, furthered this interest, devoting the main part of their curriculum to classical studies.

On the other hand it has been argued with justice that within this golden period of sixteenth-century English literature there is little intrinsic to its greatness which is recognisably classical in timbre, form, or theme. Neither Sidney's sonnets nor Spenser's *Faerie Queene* can legitimately be regarded as modelling themselves on the verse of Greece or Rome. In drama, if the dramatists had learned from Seneca's unacted closet plays a taste for blood and violence, for scenes of amputated limbs and declamatory rhetoric, those were not the qualities which gave the Elizabethan stage its imaginative range and poetic splendour. On the contrary, it gained those only as it moved away from such classical tutelage into independence. As a result, C. S. Lewis, in one of the best-known studies of English literature in this period, begins his work by denying that the literary vigour achieved at this time can be attributed to the humanist revival of classical learning. It should be regarded, he argues, as simply an inexplicable phenomenon, the chance appearance at one time and in one country of a few individual writers of genius.[2]

The weakness of that argument is the very narrow conception of humanism on which it is based. The Renaissance was far more than a revival of classical learning or the imitation of an ancient style. It represented, rather, a complex shift in human thought of which the return to classical models was more a symptom than a cause. The early humanists, whether consciously or not, were really conducting a search for an alternative authority, also bearing the sanction of antiquity, which could serve as complement and at times as counterweight to that which had dominated the Middle Ages. The search was less for styles of writing than for new styles of thought. It was eclectic, choosing to adopt only those elements in classical philosophy or art theory which suited the requirements of the searchers, and the sixteenth-century flowering of English literature needs to be seen not merely in terms of stylistic indebtedness but within the context of those larger changes.

Those changes are not easy to define, but it can, I think, be argued that the strength of the Renaissance in all its ramifications and complexity can be traced to its extraordinary duality, its incorporation of two markedly different concepts, sometimes clashing openly within it, sometimes fruitfully intermingling, but always ensuring on the part of the writer and thinker a widened range of perception. The appearance of the Italian *rinascimento* or cultural 'rebirth' may have seemed sudden to those experiencing it at the time as it reached its peak around 1500, but it was in fact the culmination of movements originating as early as the thirteenth century. In that earlier period, it had been universally assumed that Christian humility demanded from the scholar a reverential acceptance of respected sources. The mind of the medieval scholar, sharp as it might be in arguing points of theology, was not attuned to questioning received information. Thomas Aquinas, in his *Summa Contra Gentiles* (1259—64), mentions as if it were an indisputable fact the existence of a fish called a *remora* which, although only eighteen inches long, was supposed to possess the mysterious power of immobilising the largest of ships. Now, however, there appeared the first signs of a change. Roger Bacon, attacking such blind acceptance of untested tradition, began in the thirteenth century to insist that such facts be verified by a study of nature. Only by experiment, he argued, could the truth be known. A little later William of Ockham, resisting the prevailing faith in universals, posited a Nominalist philosophy in which he accorded validity only to the single, verifiable object, thereby opening a path, in an age which had always given primacy to theological truth, for the pursuit of scientific research.

The effects of the scientific revolution to which it eventually led were not to be fully felt until the seventeenth century, but that new interest in the isolated fact, the object as it really is, was enormously relevant for our period. It led in the arts to a new concern with the accurate rendering of material substances and objects. There is a careful painting of a rabbit in the corner of an *Annunciation* by Giovanni di Paolo, a lively interest in the details of clothing as a mark of social status in the manuscript illustrations of the Limbourg brothers, and, by their contemporary, Chaucer, an amused description of the small coral 'gauded all with green' on the arm of the Prioress, as well as her brooch of shining gold on which a flourishing *A* introduces the inappropriate motto *Amor vincit omnia*.

The significance of this empirical tendency is that it marked one extreme within a polarised view of the world. The opposite pole found its fullest expression in the teachings of Marsilio Ficino. In a villa near Florence presented to him in 1462 by Cosimo de' Medici, he founded an academy devoted to Plato's teachings. The group of devotees he gathered about him was more of a cult than a scholarly academy. A lamp was left permanently burning before a bust of Plato, celebrations were held in honour of his birthday, and hymns sung in his praise. But the votaries did also engage

in serious scholarship, and under Ficino's guidance the
dialogues of Plato were translated into Latin in order to
ensure their wider dissemination, as were the works of
Plotinus and others. Of greater consequence was the creation
there of a revived form of Neoplatonism remarkably congenial
to the needs of that age, a merger of Platonism and Christianity
which was to serve as a bridge from the Middle Ages to the
new world. According to that philosophy, although man
belonged within the material world, his soul was held to
participate in the divine. No longer seen as doomed from
birth by original sin and utterly dependent upon God's grace,
here the human soul held within its power the ability to
ascend by reason and by love (its yearning for the celestial)
until it finally reached the realm of the divine itself. By
becoming part of the godly, it was endowed also with the
ability to create, so that the merely skilful craftsman of the
past now achieved an elevated status, as the 'divine' artist or
poet of the new era. His task was to produce the universal
harmonies of art. More generally, man, by clothing the
particular in this world in its spiritual or allegorical meaning,
could now soar into the universal, towards the ideal 'Beautiful-
and-Good' identified with God himself.

Here, then, were two extrapolated views. On the one hand,
a sober empirical insistence upon the provable fact or object,
and on the other a movement away from physical reality
towards a concept of man unbounded in his abilities and
reaching up to the universal ideals in heaven itself. Sometimes
the views drift far apart, and seem utterly alien. Pico della
Mirandola, in his oration *Of the Dignity of Man* (1486),
urged his contemporaries to devote themselves only to the
celestial: 'Let us disdain earthly things, strive for heavenly
things, and finally, esteeming less whatever belongs to this
world, hasten to that court which is beyond the world and
nearest to the Godhead.' Against his view is set the harsh
pragmatism of Machiavelli's *The Prince* (1513), which cuts
through the mists of moral idealism to see the actuality of
power politics in the Italian states as he had witnessed them.
The age might talk nobly of ethical responsibility in leader-
ship, of Christian charity, of the need to love one's fellow
man, but the facts spoke differently. The only way Machiavelli
himself had seen princes like Cesar Borgia (the latter had

assassinated his own brother and murdered all possible successors) gain power and hold on to it effectively was by ruthless cunning and cynical self-interest. Accordingly, the advice he offers any aspiring political leader is to follow where the historical and tangible facts point, irrespective of moral scruples.

So much for the dichotomy. But in art and literature of the time that duality of concept, the idealistic and the pragmatic, when enrichingly integrated, provided the artist with an amazing range, a vision of man reaching as high as the heavens, yet still rooted in this tactile earth. The Renaissance hero is seen as rivalling the gods themselves in splendour, yet tripping through some small factual error of human judgement, a moment's thoughtlessness, a minor spot or blemish which corrupts his virtues, be they as pure as grace. He may command the storms in his wrath, yet at the same time is seen realistically as no more than a poor, forked animal, vulnerable to rain and cold, and succumbing at the last to the cold touch of death. In a speech of wider significance than his own specific dilemma, Hamlet epitomises that vision in all its grandeur and in all its melancholy:

> What a piece of work is man, how noble in reason, how infinite in faculties, in form and moving how express and admirable, in action how like an angel, in apprehension how like a god: the beauty of the world, the paragon of animals; and yet to me what is this quintessence of dust?   [II, ii]

This is not the medieval view that in the midst of life we are in death, for ever reminding man that this world is as nothing, a shadowy anteroom before the Day of Judgement. On the contrary, it is an assertion of man's magnificent potential, his infinite faculties, his godlike apprehension; but offset by the sobering fact of his physical limitations. The only tangible evidence remaining after his noble achievements in this world is the putrefying flesh in the grave and the nauseating stench of a decaying skull. The astonishing poetic and dramatic spectrum offered by this twofold vision, the empirical and the spiritual, made possible for the era the breadth and range of its artistic productions.

The duality operates in the visual arts too and it may be helpful to glance there briefly before turning to literature. As painting deserts the medieval tradition, there emerges throughout Europe a new interest in physical reality, a concern with carefully recording the details of the natural world as they actually are. Van Eyck catches exactly the reflection of an orange in a convex mirror, Dürer painstakingly pictures every blade of grass, every thistle-spur and stalk growing within a tiny patch of ground, and Leonardo da Vinci, long before the appearance of Vesalius' anatomical charts, dissects over thirty corpses in order to determine the precise positioning of muscles, arteries and tissues for his depiction on canvas of the human form. After an age which had presented the world in terms of eternity and symbol, artists now constructed machines to allow them to plot perspective accurately, and provide on canvas the representation of a scene as the eye would actually perceive it. Yet, integrated with this determination for factual accuracy and correct architectural perspective, there develops in tandem an increasing tendency towards idealisation, taking its model from classical philosophy and practice.

In ancient Greece, Plato, relying upon Pythagoras' discovery that music was dependent on fixed mathematical ratios which produced harmonious chords, deduced the existence of universal laws prevailing throughout nature to ensure the preservation of perfect concord and culminating at the highest level in the music of the spheres. Now in the fifteenth century, the renowned humanist and architect, Leon Battista Alberti revealed that Roman architects had themselves carefully conformed to those Pythagorean proportions in designing their buildings so that the comparative size and relative positioning of the walls, doorways and columns should create a visually unified whole. In his *De re aedificatoria* (1452) he formulated the new principles for his age. The true work of art, he argued, must participate in this higher order. It must constitute a perfect, harmonious whole from which nothing can be subtracted, nothing altered without damaging its unity. Following his lead, artists now began sketching out circles, squares, and intersecting parabolas to serve as the substructures for their canvases and frescoes. Even the sketch of a face would have measured lines superimposed upon it in the early stages to ensure that the individual features should conform to the correct proportions and attain the ideal concept of beauty. Painting was thereby elevated in this era from mere visual representation into a participation in celestial harmony.

The striving for factual accuracy on the one hand and the trend towards an idealised harmony on the other, contrary as they may appear, joined forces to create that form of art specific to the High Renaissance. Where an earlier painting by Cimabue or Duccio would place the suffering Madonna against a background of gold in the stylised tradition of the ikon, da Vinci's *Madonna of the Rocks* adopts a different technique. The scene presented is dreamlike, a haunting glimpse of celestial beauty where, in accordance with Alberti's dictum, the figures are so perfectly placed in relation to each other that the slightest change would disturb the overall harmony. Yet the scene, despite its rarified sanctity remains realistically within this world. The rocks of the grotto are true geological formations, the plants and shrubs, the drape of the voluminous cloak, the fall of the curled hair utterly convincing, bringing the dream vision into conjunction with the tangible world as we know it.[3] In the same way, Michelangelo's sculptural group *Pietà* so idealises the Madonna that she appears there as a beautiful young girl, no older than the dead son lying before her. The artist here is aiming at a heightened concept of perfect beauty, if necessary at the expense of historical truth; and yet the beauty both of the mother and the son is an utterly human beauty, the beauty of astonishingly real flesh, with veins branching along the dead Christ's arm, a fold of cloth caught between two fingers, and the shape of the Madonna's rounded breasts visible through the loose and magnificently draped garment she wears. Instead of drifting away from the world into some impossibly heavenly perfection, the Renaissance artist integrates the two concepts, linking man with the elevated and celestial, while leaving him rooted in this earth.

Within our period, that ambivalence of a sharply actualised reality contrasting with, complementing, and merging with the nobly idealised vision is a primary source of achievement in all genres of literature. The following chapters will be examining these genres in detail, so that only a brief sketch of that interaction need be offered here. In romance, for example, the two worlds are sometimes partially separated, sometimes intimately joined, but they are never completely divorced. Shakespeare's *Merchant of Venice* provides us with two settings. Belmont, the home of Portia, is the golden palace of flowing wealth, of ideal generosity and wit, where dreams come true and magic caskets unite deserving lovers; against it is set the harshly realistic city of Venice, ruled by contracts and the vicissitudes of trade, where Shylock demands his pound of flesh and his legal claim must be enforced by the Duke to protect the commercial standing of the city. But the two polarised settings meet and blend as Portia comes from that dream world to bring the quality of mercy and true justice which must be made to prevail in the world of actuality, with the marriage of Bassanio to Portia symbolising the wedding of those two worlds. In poetry too, Spenser's *Faerie Queene* may suggest an imaginary world of medieval knights fighting impossibly evil monsters but the epic takes its force from our awareness throughout that those knights and monsters are in fact our own noble aspirations battling with sinful impulse and the vivid clarity of description intensifies its actuality. Moreover, to highlight its relevance to his own times, he projects into that allegorical world recognisable figures drawn from the Elizabethan court he knew at first hand, thus tying it into the real world. Sidney too, in the midst of a sonnet idealising his mistress in elevated Petrarchan terms will, unlike his mentor, unhesitatingly insert a few contemptuous thrusts at her real-life husband who stands between him and the consummation of his love. And Marlowe's Dr Faustus, revelling in the limitless power afforded him by magic, uses it 'to prove cosmography', to measure the coasts and kingdoms of this earth, and to grasp Helen of Troy in his own arms.

These are the qualities which lend such distinction to poetry and drama in the late sixteenth century. Other periods have offered elevated views of man's spiritual and imaginative yearnings, as did the Romantic poets in later years; but Wordsworth's response to the beauty of nature and its effect upon man's soul excludes completely, as if it were non-existent, the vicious realities of bird and beast tearing each other apart. The twentieth century, in contrast, sees that cruelty only too clearly in both man and beast, but it has on the other hand lost the vision of splendour; it no longer believes in man's ability to reach to the divine. The Renaissance writer at his best embraces both worlds. He possesses an acute awareness of the handling of a ship's tackle, the technicalities of falconry, the materialistic greed of man; but with it he has a sense too of the celestial harmonies to which man may attain, of human possibilities infinite in their range.

Some historians have attempted to separate the two elements, to speak as E.M.W. Tillyard did, of an Elizabethan world-picture consisting of hierarchy and moral order, in which Machiavelli's philosophy is merely an awkward anomaly. Hiram Haydn, in contrast, seeing that anomaly as more intrinsic to the age, isolated the group to which such sceptics as Montaigne belonged together with the Machiavels as being a 'Counter-Renaissance', militating against the major movement.[4] But to divorce the two elements is, I think, to deprive the era of its most splendid quality, the dynamic interplay between an ennobling sense of man's infinite possibilities in his ascent to the divine and a sharply pragmatic awareness of the realities within the human condition. Such duality produces the drama of Othello, dreaming of a love far excelling a world of purest chrysolite, set against a ruthless Iago, shrewdly putting money in his purse.

2

In search of a prose style

THE main tide of humanism did not reach England until the
early sixteenth century, and even then it advanced slowly,
one obstacle to its progress being the state of the English
language. French had long been, with Latin, the language
of international diplomacy, and Italian, with a tradition
reaching back uninterruptedly to the period of ancient Rome,
possessed the range and vocabulary requisite for the various
genres of literature. But English remained in many ways
unformed. The distinguished literature it had produced,
including the poetry of Chaucer and, more recently, the
prose of Sir Thomas Malory's *Morte Darthur* (1470), had
relied for its effect on a simplicity and directness of style
which English even in its less developed form was able to
supply. Queen Guenever's parting from Launcelot is moving
in its elemental purity of diction, employing mainly monosyllabic words in a series of loosely joined and unsubordinated
sentences:

> Therefore, Sir Launcelot, go to thy realm, and there take thee a
> wife, and live with her with joy and bliss, and I pray thee heartily
> pray for me to our Lord, that I may amend my mis-living. Now,
> sweet madam, said Sir Launcelot, would ye that I should return
> again unto my country, and there wed a lady? Nay, madam, wit you
> well that shall I never do; for I shall never be so false to you of that I
> have promised.   [XXI, ix].

Such language, perfectly fitted to its narrative context here,
was a tool as yet unsuited for hewing out sophisticated
philosophical ideas or the rolling periods of great oratory;
and the lack was sorely felt. Translation was hampered.
Castiglione's widely read *The Courtier*, published in Italy in
1528, had already appeared in Spanish by 1534 and in
French by 1538, yet it was to take thirty-three years before

the first English translation by Sir Thomas Hoby became available in 1561. Though read in the Italian by educated Englishmen before then, it could not be absorbed into the life-blood of English literature nor contribute to its prose tradition until the latter part of the century when the serious work of translation into English began, and North, Holinshed, Golding and others at last made the major classical and continental works available to all.

Moreover, English had remained markedly regional as a language, with strong overtones of local dialect. At court, even in the latter part of the century the Queen's English was by no means universal. Sir Walter Ralegh 'spake broad Devonshire to his dying day', and how far local pronunciation deviated from what was eventually to become the norm is suggested by the spelling of the time which, as yet unsystematised, reflected the actual sound of the words. The Marchioness of Exeter concludes a letter to her son ' . . . by your loving mother Gertrude Exeter' but writes '. . . by your *lowfyng* mothar, Gartrude Exet*tar*' [author's italics].[5] The setting up of Caxton's printing press in Westminster in 1476, although it produced mainly late-medieval works and therefore contributed little to the dissemination of humanism, did help towards the standardisation of spelling, and hence pronunciation, in accordance with the prevailing London dialect, but progress was slow.

The need for a more sophisticated prose, both in range of vocabulary and in more complex sentence structure, is indicated by the changed curriculum introduced into the schools by leading scholars during the first half of the century. John Colet, in founding St Paul's school in 1509, encouraged the teaching of classical literature for the value of its form even though, as a churchman and dean of the cathedral, he recognised the danger of its pagan content. Accordingly the boys there, as in all grammar schools in the country, began concentrating the major part of their studies on the improvement of their style, translating from Latin into English and then back again into Latin, endeavouring to preserve in both versions the formal elegance of the Latin model. Numerous textbooks on rhetoric began to appear in the following decades, and Richard Sherry's *A Treatise of Schemes and Tropes* (1550) confirmed the general view that

Cicero's *De Oratore* was, together with Quintilian, the best model for prose because of its 'high' style of eloquence and its rich vocabulary. ' . . . for it hath an ample majesty, very garnished words . . . and grave sentences.' These were precisely the elements which were felt to be lacking in the English prose of the day.

This educational innovation, effective as it was in moulding the style of the next generation of writers, was in itself an expression of a trend already recognisable among the scholars who had introduced the change. A comparison of the two most substantial Latin—English dictionaries produced in the fifteenth century, *Promptorium Parvulorum* (1440) and *Catholicon Anglicum* (1499) reveals that in the years between them a shift was already taking place, with the latter volume offering a much wider range of weighty Latinate words in English, such as 'confabulation' and 'taciturnity', reflecting under early humanistic influence a growing desire for classical sophistication and expanded vocabulary within the English language.[6] By the middle of the sixteenth century the movement had grown to such proportions that protests began to be raised against the exaggerated importation of what Thomas Wilson's *Art of Rhetoric* (1553) called 'inkhorn' terms, that is, words introduced merely to display the writer's erudition. He offers in that work an amusing parody of the new vogue of writing which, he insists, he has heard many people praise extravagantly. The supposed epistle begins:

Pondering, expending, and revoluting with myself your ingent affability and ingenious capacity for mundane affairs, I cannot but celebrate and extol your magnifical dexterity above all other. For how could you have adepted such illustrate prerogative and dominical superiority if the fecundity of your ingeny had not been so fertile and wonderful pregnant?

Understandably, Sir John Cheke, the Regius Professor of Greek at Cambridge, wrote in a letter to the translator Hoby: 'I am of opinion that our own tongue should be written clear and pure, unmixed and unmangled with borrowing from other tongues, wherein, if we take not heed by time, ever borrowing and never paying, she shall fain to keep her house bankrupt.'

However inappropriate the image of bankruptcy here (no country has to repay loan words), the sentiment is clear; the purity of the English language both in style and vocabulary must be protected against corruption. The danger was not only in the use of imported words, but also the often mindless imitation of Ciceronian triplets, substituting mere tautology for the powerfully incremental repetitions of the original. Berners, in the preface of his translation of Froissart (1523) argues, in a series of pointless synonyms, that historians ' . . . show, open, manifest, and declare to the reader, by example of old antiquity, what we should enquire, desire, and follow, and also what we should eschew, avoid, and utterly fly.'

However, to side with the purists in the controversy as if they were the noble defendants of the English heritage is to misunderstand the subtle changes taking place. The more perceptive critics, such as Wilson, while they justifiably scoffed at the indiscriminate use of Latinate words solely for a display of supposed scholarship, did at the same time welcome their importation as a much-needed enrichment of the language. For in the development of English prose in the sixteenth century, the new flexibility and variety of the language arose from a judicious blending of the simpler native forms with the more ornate 'eloquence' learned primarily from classical sources and to a lesser extent from French and Italian.

Style at its best is always organically related to content, and that blending of basic Anglo-Saxon forms with the more elaborate syntax of classical rhetoric was integral to the duality of Renaissance modes discussed in the previous chapter. By nature, the simpler, often monosyllabic vocabulary of earlier English was more suited to the accurate rendering of the factual and everyday, while the newly imported classical tradition, with its wealth of abstract nouns and more complex, rhythmic structures could express more effectively the loftier, sophisticated concepts. Time and again in the best prose of this period we find the more abstract or generalised philosophical discussion brought sharply to earth by a factual analogy or concrete illustration; and for the latter the language shifts back stylistically to the older more elemental forms:

Augmentation of honour and substance . . . not only impresseth a reverence, whereof proceedeth due obedience among subjects but also inflameth men naturally inclined to idleness or sensual appetite to covet like fortune, and for that cause to dispose them to study or occupation. Now to conclude my first assertion or argument, where all thing is commune, there lacketh order; and where order lacketh, there all thing is odious and uncomely. And that have we in daily experience; for the pans and pots garnisheth well the kitchen, and yet should they be to the chamber none ornament. Also the beds, testers, and pillows beseemeth not the hall, no more than the carpets and cushions becometh the stable.[7]

Basically, it was the same technique as Francis Bacon was to use so tellingly at the end of the century, the contrast between an arrestingly simple opening sentence — 'Men fear death as children fear to go in the dark' — monosyllabic, factual, and unelaborated — and the subsequent rising in tone and Latinate resonance as the argument develops its broader philosophical theme.

Sir Thomas More

The mingling of classical forms with native English diction is exemplified in the writings of Sir Thomas More (1478–1535), often called England's first true humanist. He indeed deserved that title for the combining of his broad intellectual pursuits with their translation into active and public terms as a learned theologian, a secular jurist, a tolerant and perceptive observer of contemporary affairs, who was eventually to take his place as Lord Chancellor of England under Henry VIII. In a deeper sense, however, he marks rather the transition between the old world and the new, a man who, though stepping boldly into the sixteenth century as an involved participant in secular human activities, cherished, often secretively, an abiding loyalty to the cloistered asceticism of the medieval monastery. What endeared him to all who knew him was the combination in his character of the best qualities of both spheres — the ready wit, classical learning, and intellectual curiosity of the humanist with the personal humility, incorruptibility, and self-abnegation of the religious recluse.

Born to a London lawyer, More was sent as a boy to join the household of John Morton, Archbishop of Canterbury, where he distinguished himself by his ready humour and wit, traits which were to accompany him throughout his life, even to the steps of the scaffold. From Morton's household he proceeded to Oxford, responding warmly to the new humanist trends, and thence to law studies in London. More's career now appeared assured, when unexpectedly he turned his back on the world. In 1499 he entered the Charterhouse in London, at that time a monastery belonging to the austere Carthusian order. There for a period of four years he lived in seclusion, though without as yet taking vows, and from a remark made towards the end of his life it would seem that part of him always yearned to return. At the end of that four-year period his confessor, Dean Colet, persuaded him that his task lay in the world outside, and he was urged by him to marry and set up a household.

The household he established was a model of its kind, with encouragement for every form of useful study and discussion. After one visit, his life-long friend Erasmus compared it enthusiastically to Plato's academy ' . . . yet more rightly to a school for Christian religion.' In women's liberation, More marked a considerable advance for his time, educating his daughters so well that they became famed for their learning. Yet, although he had moved out of the monastery into the secular world of marriage and career, the change did not go as deep as might appear; for beneath his doublet and gold chain of office, certainly during his years as Chancellor and possibly before then too, he wore unknown to all but his eldest daughter the rough hair-shirt of a monk.

In 1513, More composed, possibly for political reasons, a brief *History of Richard III* which, although only published years later in a mutilated form, was to serve as a primary source for Holinshed and, through him, for some of the most vivid scenes in Shakespeare's play of that name. Based upon a Latin version perhaps by Archbishop Morton (which would account for the eye-witness effect) yet emerging in the English form as a work in its own right, it marks, as did More's own life, a turning-point between the old and the new. The medieval idea of history as a collection of unsubstantiated legends is replaced here by a responsible search for accuracy. He distinguishes carefully between verified information and what may be mere hearsay, reported, as he says, by 'men of hatred' towards the king. The result, however, is not a drily factual account, but a powerful and lively portrait in which the language of the prose leaps forward from the older Malory-like forms still preserved here in the narrative sections ('for well they wist that the queen was too wise to go about any such folly') to a dramatic intensity and imaginative force at the climactic moments, boding well for the future of the English theatre. Richard III is described as racked by guilt after his murder of the two young princes in the Tower:

> Where he went abroad, his eyes whirled about, his body privily fenced, his hand ever on his dagger, his countenance and manner like one alway ready to strike again; he took ill rest at nights, lay long waking and musing, sore wearied with care and watch, rather slumbered than slept, troubled with fearful dreams, suddenly sometime start up, leap out of his bed, and run about the chamber, so was his restless heart continually tossed and tumbled with the tedious impression and stormy remembrance of his abominable deed.

More's most famous work *Utopia* (1516) lies technically outside the range of this present volume since it was written in Latin. It was, however, so widely read in England both in the original and in the English translation published in 1551 by Ralph Robinson that it cannot be ignored, particularly in view of the literary offspring it fathered, including Bacon's *New Atlantis*, Swift's *Gulliver's Travels*, and Samuel Butler's *Erewhon*. The work resulted from a six-month visit on an embassy to the Low Countries which serve as the locale for the discussions in the book, and in the tradition of the Platonic dialogue he mingles true with fictional characters. His use of Latin recalls once again the dilemma of the scholar at this time, needing to choose between the wider range of educated readers on the continent and the more parochial audience at home.

The first of the two books is a perceptive survey of England's moral and economic ills, often sounding remarkably modern in its suggestions for change. He attacks the cruelty of rack-renting and the enclosing of sheep-grazing land, the ostentatious extravagance of the wealthy, and the unjust penalty of death for stealing, in a society which had deprived the poor of their livelihood. All this More places very prudently in a period some twelve years before Henry VIII's accession to the throne, lest it should be interpreted as an attack on the King's command of the country.

The second part, with its account of the country of Utopia is the more famous. In More's day, the utopia of which men dreamed nostalgically was the mythological golden age of the past, the classical version of Eden before the Fall, when the conditions of man's life were ideal and the earth yielded its fruits in abundance. As a humanist, More turned from the idyllic conditions of such imaginary existence to this world, enquiring how man could create in it a viable society by relying on his own rational faculties. For its topical setting, therefore, he uses the voyages of discovery undertaken by explorers in his own day and the supposed visit of one such traveller to a country existing across the seas. If the country of Utopia ('No-place') is an acknowledged fiction, its description serves throughout as an ironic commentary on the shortcomings and irrationalities of contemporary European society, and it is that which is being explored rather than Utopia itself.

In that distant country, we learn, there is no indolent aristocracy living off the labour of the poor as in his own land, everyone being employed there in productive work. Ownership of property is equal, with houses reallocated by lot every ten years; and gold, while preserved as payment for foreign mercenaries should war be unavoidable, is kept in the form of chamber-pots and slave-rings so that wealth should be despised by the citizens. While marriage is encouraged, extra-marital intercourse is severely punished (with the rather sour justification that few would tolerate the trials of marriage were sexual activity permitted outside it), and both divorce and remarriage are permitted, the latter not for proven adulterers who have shown their inability to function correctly within the marital framework.

So brief a summary can only offer the bare bones of what is an extraordinarily witty and stimulating account, brimming over with novel ideas; and its very unconventionality has led to markedly different interpretations. For some critics More is seen as the forefather of modern socialism, distributing the country's wealth to ensure the greatest happiness of the greatest number. Others perceive in the work the very reverse, a return to medievalism, whereby Utopia becomes (with the exception of marriage) one large monastery with everyone forced to wear the same rough habit, to eat communally with meals preceded by instructive readings, to have their hours regulated, and property held in common. What, moreover, has troubled many readers is the contradiction between the principles advocated by the book and the religious convictions held by More himself. *Utopia* permits euthanasia under certain conditions, allows women to become priests, and approves of divorce and remarriage, all in direct contravention of basic tenets in the Catholic church; and this quite apart from milder suggestions upon which the church would undoubtedly frown, such as the requirement that prospective marriage partners should always examine each other naked before finally plighting their troth.

Part of the answer, but not all, lies in More's teasing tone which often undercuts his own seriousness and leaves the reader unsure where the author's real commitment rests. The narrator who admiringly describes the Utopia he has visited is named Hythloday ('A talker of nonsense'), the king is Ademus ('Without a people'), and More, who appears as a participant in the discussion, on occasion expresses his own disagreement with the arguments his own book presents. In real life More was known for his poker-faced jesting, once being charged: 'You use . . . to look so sadly when you mean merrily that many times men doubt whether you speak in sport when you mean good earnest'; and allowance must be made for that humorous vein within the account. On the other hand, as its impact on its era and on subsequent generations has shown, the book deals too seriously with matters of great moment for it to be dismissed as a mere joke.

Perhaps the true answer is to be found in the dichotomy within More's own personality, the rationalist committed to a religious faith with a hair-shirt concealed beneath his humanist garb. It may well be that in this book he is indulging his intellect, allowing the humanist side of his character to range freely, temporarily released from the restrictions of his faith, in order to speculate as a Renaissance thinker how in a country as yet untouched by Christianity man might use the resources of his reason to establish rules of social and moral behaviour without the aid of divine imperatives. Utopia would be for him, then, the 'green world' of Shakespeare's plays, a mythical country in which the imagination can roam at large, untroubled by personal commitments, before returning to this world with the moral insights it has gained.

In his later writings, the theologian in him took precedence, but even then he laced his prose with wit and humorous anecdote. He attacked Tyndale in his *Dialogue Concerning Heresies* (1529) and in resisting a move to have church property confiscated, in his *Supplication of Souls* published in the same year, instead of solemnly attacking the move he puckishly draws a picture of past donors gathering mournfully in purgatory to beg that they be not deprived of the prayers promised for the gifts they had bestowed. More had now become so eminent a figure on the European scene that his refusal to countenance Henry VIII's claim to the Supremacy of the Church could not be tolerated by the King. He resigned from the Chancellorship in 1532 and two years later was arrested and tried for treason on the grounds that he would not take the new oath of allegiance. His ability as a jurist and perhaps also as a humorist did not desert him even at such a time: he argued with tongue in cheek that since silence means consent, his refusal to take the oath should be regarded as perfectly satisfactory. But the decision had already gone against him before the trial began. While imprisoned in the Tower he composed his *Dialogue of Comfort Against Tribulation*, a devotional work whose prose style, generally more weighty and solemn than his earlier works, is enlivened repeatedly by homely images which contrast with the general tone by their simple forms of expression:

> . . . he that in tribulation turneth himself into worldly vanities to get help and comfort from them, fareth like a man that in peril of drowning catcheth whatsoever cometh next to hand, and that holdeth he fast be it never so simple a stick, but then that helpeth him not. For that stick he draweth under the water with him, and there lie they drowned both together.

Towards the end of his imprisonment he was deprived of writing materials, but from *The Life of More* written by his son-in-law William Roper in the 1550s we learn how, on being told that the King whom he had served so faithfully had ordered his execution, he replied to the courtier with gentle sarcasm:

> I have always been much bound to the King's Highness for the many benefits and honours that he hath still from time to time most

bountifully heaped upon me; especially that it hath pleased his Majesty to put me here in this place where I have had convenient time and leisure to remember my last end; and now most of all am I bound unto his Grace, that I shall so shortly be rid out of the miseries of this wretched life.

Educated governors

The eminent scholars surrounding More, such as William Grocyn, John Colet, and Thomas Linacre, had by their enthusiastic dedication to learning, succeeded in transplanting to English soil the seeds of Florentine humanism; but they were not themselves literary figures. It fell to the lot of a younger member of that circle, Sir Thomas Elyot (c. 1490– 1546), to produce what was perhaps the first literary work in English which both advocated and exemplified the New Learning. His early career had only advanced him to the office of Clerk of the King's Council, an unpaid post of which he was deprived when his patron Wolsey fell from power. Only partially consoled by the award of a knighthood in lieu of more tangible renumeration, he withdrew to his country manor where he turned his attention to writing. The work he produced, *The Book Named the Governor* (1531), which achieved immediate success and went into eight editions before 1580, marked the introduction into England of the so-called 'courtesy' book, the guide to a gentleman's education.

The title derives from the specific meaning he bestows on the term 'governor'. Unlike More, Elyot did not believe in the possibility of a classless society. All nature, he maintained, is constructed on hierarchical principles, and in human society too an all-powerful monarch must of necessity stand at the head of the state or 'weal' (hence the book's dedication to Henry VIII, and the favour it found in royal eyes). Such a ruler, however capable he may be, cannot govern unaided, but requires immediately below him a stratum of magistrates or lesser 'governors' to implement the laws of the realm. The concern of his book is the nurturing of such a class.

The significance of education in the overall humanist programme can scarcely be overestimated. Under the feudal system of the Middle Ages, sons of the aristocracy were sent (as More had been) to serve as pages in another household, where they acquired by daily experience rather than by any planned course of study the attributes of a courtier, their only formal lessons being in the arts of reading and writing. The humanism which More had met later, on attending the university, made heavier demands. It assumed as axiomatic, the perfectability, or at least the near-perfectability of man. Let a gentleman be thoroughly grounded from childhood in classical literature, let him study the actions of great men of history, learning from their achievements and their failings, let him develop a sensitivity to poetry, music, and art, and he would emerge as the all-round civilised man capable of ruling with 'magnanimity' in the broad Roman sense of that term. Today we are perhaps more sceptical of the effects of education, but in its day the system did produce such distinguished personalities as Federigo di Montefeltro in whose elegant court at Urbino the painter Raphael was reared, and in England under the tutelage of Roger Ascham a queen who amazed foreign visitors by her fluency in French, Italian, Spanish, and Latin, her comprehension of the responsibilities of high office, her intimidating command of administrative detail, and not least her ability to cultivate about her a court in which music, poetry, theatre, and dance could flourish in a manner rarely, if ever, equalled in other eras.

Elyot justifiably deplored the contempt for learning prevalent in his day among members of the upper class. Scholarship was still associated with the threadbare university 'clerk' as Chaucer had described him, so that, Elyot complained, 'to a great gentleman it is a notable reproach to.be well learned and to be called a great clerk.' It is largely to the credit of Elyot and his fellow humanists that the attitude changed so fundamentally during the century and learning became an indispensable part of the fashionable courtier's accoutrements. With that change came a rise in the status of the schoolmaster or private tutor. Elyot scorns noblemen who expend more care and money in choosing their cook than in selecting the educator of their offspring, and are satisfied with some poorly trained bachelor of arts who imparts a superficial knowledge 'which will be washed off with the first rain.' Instead he demands the highest qualifications, summarising, in effect, the ideal schoolmaster of the new era, and placing his emphasis too on classical training and stylistic analysis. He must be one:

> . . . that speaking Latin elegantly, can expound good authors, expressing the invention and disposition of the matter, their style or form of eloquence, explicating the figures as well of sentences as words, leaving no thing, person, or place named by the author undeclared or hidden from his scholars. Wherefore Quintilian saith, it is not enough for him to have read poets, but all kinds of writing must also be sought for: not for the histories only, but also for the propriety of words.

The requirement for propriety of words he extends from Latin composition to include English prose too, and his choice of English rather than Latin as the vehicle for his treatise was, as he remarked in later years, a conscious attempt 'to augment the English tongue.' His decision set a precedent, helping to wean subsequent writers away from Latin to their native English. The care he shows for propriety of words in his own writing reveals an awareness on his part that English vocabulary was in need of enrichment, and accordingly he generally prefers a longer Latinate word such as *commendation* or *decoction* where a simple word would do as well. The result is a prose often weightier than the content requires, although the firm sentence structure and controlled rhythms help to counteract this failing and to ensure an overall clarity of meaning. A typical passage runs:

> Although I have hitherto advanced the commendation of learning, specially in gentlemen, yet it is to be considered that continual study without some manner of exercise shortly exhausteth the spirits vital and hindereth natural decoction and digestion, whereby man's body is the sooner corrupted and brought into divers sicknesses, and finally the life is thereby made shorter; where contrariwise by exercise, which is a vehement motion . . . the health of man is preserved, and his strength increased.

He was a pioneer of the new prose rather than an accomplished stylist, but he did possess one quality rare in this period, a flexibility of style enabling him to adapt to the needs of his subject. In illustrating the virtue of amity, he retells with masterly skill the tale of Titus and Gisippus from Boccaccio, deserting the formal rhetoric of his treatise in

favour of a lighter diction and smoother-flowing sentence out
of which the later Elizabethan narratives were to develop:

> But at last the pain became so intolerable, that could he or no, he
> was enforced to keep his bed, being for lack of sleep and other
> sustenance brought in such feebleness that his legs might not sustain
> his body. Gisippus missing his dear friend Titus was much abashed,
> and hearing that he lay sick in his bed had forthwith his heart
> pierced with heaviness, and with all speed came to where he lay.

The programme he designs for the education of the young
nobleman is, in accordance with the new humanist trends,
strongly inclined towards the classics both in the historical
figures selected for emulation and in the writers who are to
serve as models. As a result, the ideal to which the programme
aspires approximates to the Roman *virtus* rather than the
traditional Christian virtues. There are brief nods in the
direction of the Bible and the Church Fathers, but it is clear
that Alexander the Great, Hannibal, and Mark Antony have
begun to replace as models for behaviour the lives of Francis
of Assisi and the patron saints.

In the same year as the book appeared, with its dedication
to Henry VIII, its author was rewarded by an appointment as
ambassador to the court of Emperor Charles V; but he
continued his literary activities, publishing numerous translations from the classics, a dialogue in Platonic style, and in
1538 the first major Latin—English dictionary incorporating
the New Learning, which in an enlarged form served scholars
throughout the Elizabethan era. His layman's guide to good
health based upon Galen and entitled *The Castle of Health*
proved even more popular than his educational treatise and
reached fifteen editions by the turn of the century. It has
little literary value but is a valuable source-book for sixteenth-
century views on hygiene, diet, the humours, and the peculiar
mingling of fact and fantasy which constituted medical practice in that period.

Elyot had defined the ideal schoolmaster from the
viewpoint of the 'governor' class, but Roger Ascham
(1516—68) did so as an experienced teacher himself, the past
tutor of one royal scholar who, as he proudly informed her
courtiers, went 'beyond you all in excellency of learning'
and, despite her busy schedule, spent more hours studying

each day than six of them together. An outstanding classicist and a pupil of Sir John Cheke, Ascham was appointed to a readership in Greek at Cambridge, but found the payment too meagre for his needs (possibly because of an unscholarly addiction to dicing and cockfighting which, according to a contemporary, kept him poor throughout his life). Like so many of the more ambitious young men of his day, he turned his eye towards the court, to which Cheke himself had made his way as a tutor to Prince Edward. In a successful attempt to catch the King's attention, he published in 1545 a book on archery, particularly the use of the long-bow, entitled *Toxophilus*. As the long-bow was still regarded with patriotic pride as the Englishman's truest weapon in battle, the treatise found favour with Henry VIII, who awarded him an annual pension worth double his salary at Cambridge, on which presumably he could now indulge his sporting instincts more liberally.

What might have been a dull instructional booklet is so enlivened by the learned historical references, the mythological allusions, the writer's enthusiasm for his subject, and the frequent excursions into fascinating bye-ways, that it arouses the ardour of readers who have never taken a bow in hand. Ascham graphically compares the archer resisting wind-drag to a captain at the helm of his vessel. 'The master of a ship first learneth to know the coming of a tempest, the nature of it, and how to behave himself in it, either with changing his course, or pulling down his tops and broad sails, being glad to eschew as much of the weather as he can: even so a good archer will first with diligent use and marking the weather, learn to know the nature of the wind, and with wisdom, will measure in his mind how much it will alter his shot, either in length keeping or else in straight shooting . . . .'

The diction here is markedly simple, particularly when we recall Ascham's excellent classical background; and the simplicity was deliberate on his part. In the preface to the book, he answers those who have introduced Latin, French, and Italian words on the assumption that it will enrich the language in the same way as wine, ale, and beer improve a feast: 'Truly, quod I, they be all good, every one taken by himself alone, but if you put malvoisie and sack, red wine and white, ale and beer, and all in one pot, you shall make a drink neither easy to be known, nor yet wholesome for the body.' Similarly, he was one of the first to attack legal jargon or what he called 'indenture' English. However, although he was a conscious purist in diction, a close reading of the quotation below on wind direction will reveal how the rhythms of Latin prose have entered his style, the repetitions for rhetorical effect, the subordinate participial clauses, and the echoing of a word or phrase which together create the more intricate and sophisticated tone of the sentence. Yet, on the other hand, the simplicity of his diction lends a sharp clarity to his writing, the crispness and exactitude of his description of the varying eddies and drifts created by the wind forming part of that empirical closeness of observation which was an essential part of the Renaissance outlook. Its combination here with the emotional responsiveness on the part of the spectator elevates it far above mere factual tabulation, creating a superb piece of prose.

> That morning the sun shone bright and clear, the wind was whistling aloft and sharp according to the time of the year. The snow in the highway lay loose and trodden with horses' feet: so as the wind blew, it took the loose snow with it, and made it so slide upon the snow in the field which was hard and crusted by reason of the frost overnight, that thereby I might see very well the whole nature of the wind as it blew that day. And I had a great delight and pleasure to mark it, which maketh me now far better to remember it. Sometimes the wind would not be past two yards broad, and so it would carry the snow as far as I could see. Another time the snow would blow over half the field at once. Sometimes the snow would tumble softly, by and by it would fly wonderfully fast. And thus I perceived also that the wind goeth by streams and not whole together.

Shortly after he completed this book, his pupil William Grindal who, under his guidance, had served as Princess Elizabeth's tutor, died suddenly, and in 1548 Ascham agreed to take over the task. That move marked his entry into the English court, where he was to become a respected and influential figure. In the course of time he was appointed Edward VI's Latin secretary (the composer of official letters to foreign governments), and despite his Protestantism, continued to serve under Catholic Mary and then again under Queen Elizabeth until his death in 1568. It was in the later period that he wrote *The Schoolmaster*, published post-

humously in 1570, a book justly famed for the warm
humanity and understanding it displayed in a period when
education was still associated with the birch-rod. The wise
advice it offers is often as relevant today as it was then. He
observes, for example, that a slower pupil may not always
be inferior to the quick-witted, nor always deserving of
punishment. The teacher should consider future potential
rather than present disposition. 'For this I know, not only by
reading of books in my study, but also by experience of life
abroad in the world, that those which be commonly the
wisest, the best learned, and best men also when they be old,
were never commonly the quickest of wit when they were
young' and he analyses with great perception the reasons
which may lie behind such slowness in youth.

His gentleness and tolerance as a teacher are strangely
offset by irritable diatribes against the corruption prevalent
in Italy (now no longer viewed as the source of humanism
but as the hotbed of Catholicism), against Malory's *Morte
Darthur* in which 'those be counted the noblest knights that
do kill most men without any quarrel and commit foulest
adulteries by subtlest shifts', and against the ostentatious
apparel worn by courtiers in his day. If we may not always
accept his moral or literary criteria, there can be only admir-
ation for the force and dignity of his language, the rhetorical
power to which prose had attained during the passing decades
of the century:

> Take heed, therefore, you great ones in the Court, yea though ye be
> the greatest of all, take heed what you do, take heed how you live.
> For as you great ones use to do, so all mean men love to do. You be
> indeed makers or marrers of all men's manners within the realm. For
> though God hath placed you to be chief in making laws, to bear
> greatest authority, to command all others: yet God doth order that
> all your laws, all your authority, all your commandments do not half
> so much with mean men, as doth your manner of living.

The tone of the preacher rings out in that last passage, and
we should recall that no study of English prose can afford to
ignore the sermons of this era. In contrast to the great
preachers of a later age, such as John Donne, Dean of St
Paul's, or Bishop Launcelot Andrewes, who carefully wrote
out their sermons before delivery, the preachers of this era

generally extemporised. One of the greatest was Hugh Latimer
(*c*. 1485—1555), Bishop of Worcester who, in the purges
conducted under the Catholic Queen Mary, was to end his
life at the stake in the Protestant cause with the stirring
exhortation to his fellow martyr: 'Be of good comfort,
Master Ridley, and play the man: we shall this day light such
a candle by God's grace in England as, I trust, shall never be
put out.'

The sermons we possess by him are in all probability based
on notes taken by attentive auditors, but they convey even in
that form his extraordinary ability to grip the attention of his
listeners. There are no lengthy classical periods. The sentences
are short and to the point, dramatic in their immediacy, the
series of questions arousing curiosity, the images drawn from
the world of everyday experience. In a sermon delivered in
1548, he chides the prelates of England for failing in their
task of caring for the people, comparing them to idle ploughmen absent when the soil needs them most — 'the plough
standeth, there is no work done; the people starve.' Then he
pauses:

> And now I would ask a strange question: who is the most diligent
> bishop and prelate in all England, that passeth all the rest in doing
> his office? I can tell, for I know him who it is; I know him well. But
> now I think I see you listing and harkening that I should name him.
> There is one that passeth all the others, and is the most diligent
> prelate and preacher in all England. And will ye know who it is? I
> will tell you: it is the Devil. He is the most diligent preacher of all
> others: he is never out of his diocese; he is never from his cure; ye
> shall never find him unoccupied; he is ever in his parish: he keepeth
> residence at all times; you shall never find him out of the way. Call
> for him when you will, he is ever at home.

This passage owes little to the classics, and a phrase such as
'I know him who it is' suggests the reason. For while the
purists were protesting against the deliberate infusion of
classical and continental 'inkhorn' terms into English,
unobtrusively an additional force was at work, a further
model contributing its own rhythms and idioms to English
prose. At church services and in the daily readings customary
in many family circles, the new English translations of the
Bible were becoming familiar to the ear, their imagery,
phraseology, and cadences being gradually absorbed into the
language.

Bible translation

After the early attempts at such translation under Wycliffe in
the fourteenth century a long interval had elapsed, but the
Reformation movement gave it renewed impetus and,
through the advent of printing, vastly improved powers of
dissemination.

In England the work began inauspiciously. William
Tyndale's version of the New Testament (1526), produced on
the continent, aroused the ire of More and the English bishops
by its tendentious use of *congregation* instead of *church*,
senior instead of *priest* with their overtly Protestant implications (the Protestants were bitterly opposed to the priesthood),
and all copies of the book upon which the authorities could
lay their hands were publicly burned at St Paul's Cross.
Tyndale's earlier withdrawal across the Channel did not save
him, and in 1536 he was betrayed and executed near Brussels
as a heretic. Ironically, by the time of his execution the
climate in England had changed radically. The break with
Rome had been implemented to suit Henry VIII's marital
needs, his antagonist More had himself been put to death for
his religious views, and Henry VIII, although moving hesitantly
towards changes in dogma or ritual, had agreed to act as
patron for the complete Miles Coverdale Bible of 1535,
which incorporated much of Tyndale's own work. Three
years later, a royal decree required every church to possess its
own large copy of an English Bible for the use of parishioners
and, with only a temporary set-back under the Catholic rule
of Queen Mary (1553—8) when the translators wisely moved
to the stronghold of Calvinism in Geneva, the process of
translation proceeded in England undisturbed.

The acknowledged beauty of these translations, beginning
with Tyndale and culminating in the Authorised Version of
1611, has often been attributed to their coinciding with the
maturing of the English language, to the existence at that
time of a prose sufficiently rich and flexible to serve their
needs. The facts, however, point in a very different direction
suggesting that it was the literal translation of the Bible
which helped change the form of English prose. For a
contemporary, the fidelity to the original which the sanctity
of the scriptures required made those new versions of the
Bible foreign-sounding in English ears, the imposition of an

ancient idiom and unfamiliar cadences on the native forms of
English rather than a translation into an indigenous tongue.
Since the Reformation in many ways formed part of the
Renaissance, the ferment of activity in Bible translation had
been prompted very largely by a humanist urge for accuracy,
for the empirical testing-out of knowledge. No longer prepared
to accept the scriptures in the form in which they had been
filtered through Catholic exegesis, the Reformers were
determined to inspect the sources at first hand, to go beyond
the venerated Latin Vulgate to the original Hebrew of the
Old Testament and the Greek of the New. Fidelity to the
original was at a premium, and as a result, however natural
the rhythmic patterns and biblical phrases may appear today
after they have already been absorbed into the language, at
the time John Selden complained bitterly at their strangely
un-English form:

> There is no book so translated as the Bible. For the purpose, if I
> translate a French book into English, I turn it into English phrase
> and not into French English. *Il fait froid* I say 'it is cold', not 'it
> makes cold'; but the Bible is translated into English words rather
> than into English phrase. The Hebraisms are kept and the phrase of
> that language is kept, as for example 'he uncovered her shame',
> which is well enough so long as scholars have to do with it, but when
> it comes among the common people, Lord what gear do they make
> of it!

As knowledge of Greek and Hebrew improved during the
century, so the progressive versions of the Bible moved
against the stream of developing English prose, away from
the native English rhythms and Ciceronian rhetoric towards
more literal renderings which preserved the cadences of the
ancient original. Ciceronian prose, now fully entering the
English language, achieved its rhetorical effects by the repetition of clauses or phrases within a larger sentence, the
repetition often being threefold. Thus Ascham trusts that the
King will perceive his treatise ' . . . to be a thing honest for
me to write, pleasant for some to read, and profitable for
many to follow.' In contrast, the biblical pattern was an
oscillatory parallelism of complete sentences or ideas, an ebb
and flow in which the second half of the verse, approximately
equal in length, doubled back on the meaning of the first,

amplifying, emphasising, or particularising the earlier thought. Coverdale, relying on the Latin and German translations, although he does catch something of that rhythm, often blurs the effect, but the later Authorised Version, adhering scrupulously to a word-for-word rendering of the Hebrew, transfers the original parallelist form directly to the English tongue:

> *Coverdale*: From that time forth shall not one people lift up weapon against another, neither shall they learn to fight from thenceforth.   [Isaiah ii, 4]
> *Authorised Version*: Nation shall not lift up sword against nation, neither shall they learn war any more.

These rhythms, together with the phraseology of the Bible, became part of English prose, from the time that Coverdale's translation gave the first hints of them and with increasing effect as the versions became more literal. They are particularly recognisable at those moments when a writer temporarily dons the mantle of the prophet to speak with the authority of the scriptures. John Foxe's *The Book of Martyrs* (1563) won its wide popularity in part by its unpretentious narrative style in which were described as if by eye-witness account the dreadful sufferings of the Christian, and especially the Protestant, martyrs throughout history. As he pauses to comment on the implications of their passage from this world to the next, the prose suddenly takes fire with the fervour of the believer. The words are his own, but the parallelist cadences and idiom draw unmistakably on the scriptural source:

> The more hard the passage be, the more glorious shall they appear in the latter resurrection. Not that the afflictions of this life are worthy of such glory, but that it is God's heavenly pleasure to reward them. Never are the judgements and ways of men like unto the judgements and ways of God, but contrary evermore unless they be taught of him.

Similarly, Hugh Latimer, preaching against London, writes:

> The butterfly gloryeth not in her own deeds, nor prefereth the traditions of men before God's word; it committeth not idolatry nor worshippeth false gods. But London cannot abide to be rebuked,

such is the nature of man. If they be pricked, they will kick. If they be rubbed on the gale, they will wince. But yet they will not amend their faults, they will not be ill spoken of.

Now that England had turned away from the Roman Church, a Latin breviary or missal would no longer serve, and Cranmer's *Book of Common Prayer* (1549) was completed to take its place, henceforth accompanying English men and women to baptisms, weddings, and funerals, to divine services and private meditation, and thereby injecting into their consciousness the measured dignity of Cranmer's own versions of the prayers, interspersed with passages quoted from the Coverdale Bible. Classical influence still remained predominant in English prose at this time, but it blended with the scriptural rhythms and idioms as well as with the older simpler forms of fifteenth-century English. By the latter half of the sixteenth century, therefore, English prose could already offer a much wider range of vocabulary and rhetorical syntax as a result of the revived interest in classical, continental, and biblical sources, while preserving through the insistence of such purists as Cheke, Wilson, and Ascham (who had themselves contributed so greatly to the deepening of classical studies), the native diction and structural simplicity of earlier times.

3
The music of poetry

THE state of English poetry before the new styles were imported from Italy is vividly exemplified by the verse of that lively, caustic, and often bawdy cleric John Skelton (*c.* 1460–1529). Highly regarded in his day as poet and scholar, and a laureate of both Oxford and Cambridge universities, he was singled out for praise by Caxton and Erasmus as a leading luminary of the English literary scene. Yet within a few decades his reputation went into eclipse. His rugged verse held little appeal for the more polished age of the sonneteers, and with the appearance of an anonymous jestbook which used his name to advertise its wares, the *Merry Tales Made by Master Skelton* (1567), he began to be remembered more as a buffoon and mad-wag than as a serious poet. Only in our own century, with its rebellion against the smooth-flowing verse of the Victorians and its search for unconventional and often dissonant forms, did his 'Skeltonics' come back into favour, admired afresh for their native vigour and satirical pungency.

For a reader unacquainted with Skelton's life, the coarse ribaldry in much of his verse can be misleading. His boisterous description of a female tavern-keeper, with its earthy language and jogging rhythms, might appear to be the work of some peasant tippler with a lively imagination and a flair for rhyme:

> Droopy and drowsy,
> Scurvy and lousy,
> Her face all bowsy,*   *bloated
> Comely crinkled,
> Wondrously wrinkled,
> Like a roast pig's ear,
> Bristled with hair.
> Her lewd lips twain
> They slaver, men sain . . .

He was, in fact, a distinguished classicist, renowned for his elegant translation of many Latin works, including Cicero's letters, into an 'aureate' English prose; and the discovery in 1956 of his only surviving translation, a version of Diodorus Siculus, confirms the justice of his reputation. However, if Skelton was a classicist he was by no means a humanist. In an era marked by the revival of Greek studies, his own knowledge of that language remained negligible. He was deeply suspicious of the Reformist tendencies within the church, and actively opposed the changes being introduced into the school curriculum. His Latin scholarship was, in fact, of the old style, rooted in the late medieval tradition, and in his poetry too he harked back to the Chaucerian world in which he felt more at home. 'The Tunning of Elinor Rumming' (1517), from which the above quotation comes, has an obvious kinship with the description of the Wife of Bath, not merely as an unflattering and amusing vignette of a woman, but more fundamentally in its use of telling detail as a means of creating character. He focuses upon the bare threads in Elinor's 'huke' or cloak which she fondly imagines is as splendid as when she bought it forty years before:

> Her huke of Lincoln green,
> It had been hers, I ween,
> More than forty year,
> And so it doth appear;
> And the green bare threads
> Look like sere weeds,
> Withered like hay,
> The wool worn away.
> And yet I dare say
> She thinketh herself gay
> When she doth her array . . .

The interest in meticulous description is here, but not as yet any striving for aesthetic elevation of the scene such as was to motivate the following generation of writers and artists. There is rather a confrontation with an unadorned truth, the realism being allowed to speak for itself.

In the development of his verse-forms, Skelton moved in the opposite direction from the norm. He began with an ornate sophistication in his poetry, but in his search for more vigorous modes he gradually rejected the ornate in favour of a rough plainness, often crude in its diction as well as its rhythms. His earlier, more elaborate verse is typified by 'The Bowge of Court' ('Court Rations') of 1498. The poem is in the tradition of the allegorical dream-sequence, applied here to the falsity of court life. The court is represented as a goodly ship, richly outfitted, upon which Deceit, Dissimulation, and Disdain sail together with sundry other Vices, a technique which leans heavily upon the morality play, and the verse employed is the established seven-line stanza of rime royal, used in Chaucer's 'Troilus and Criseyde'. At the end of the poem, the speaker, appalled by what he has seen, determines to leap overboard, fleeing from such corruption. In doing so, he awakes; but lest the moral be missed, he concludes with the warning to the reader that 'ofttimes such dreams be found true'.

Skelton was in a position to speak knowledgeably of the court, having been appointed in 1489 as court poet and later as tutor of the future Henry VIII. In 1498, the year this poem was published, he took holy orders at the comparatively advanced age of thirty-eight and was soon afterwards appointed rector to the parish of Diss in Norfolk. Neither his entrance into the priesthood nor his position as rector to a Christian community seems to have restrained his penchant for ribald verse. One of his best-known poems, the lament for 'Philip Sparrow' (1508) moves towards 'Elinor Rumming' in its adoption of colloquial speech patterns. It is an elegy supposedly recited by a young girl at the loss of her favourite pet, a sparrow eaten by a cat, and the lament is cunningly intertwined with passages from the Latin Office for the Dead. It provides remarkable psychological insight into the personality of the girl, her fondness for nature, her fears of Hell's terrors, and, not least, her own erotic experiences with the bird allowed to play beneath the blanket, to which description is added her plaintive comment 'God wot, we thought no sin!' Interestingly, Skelton places in her mouth his own reasons for rejecting the new-fangled words being introduced by the humanists, and his preference for the cruder but more natural language he has adopted in his poetry. The English language, he maintains, is too weather-beaten to be renewed ('ennewed') by such importations:

Our natural tongue is rude,
And hard to be ennewed
With polished terms lusty:
Our language is so rusty,
So cankered and so full
Of frowards and so dull,
That if I were to apply
To write ordinately,
I wot not where to find
Terms to serve my mind.

and he concludes by choosing the pleasant, easy, and plain language of Chaucer.

By now his pupil Henry VIII had ascended the throne, and Skelton became embroiled in a controversy with Cardinal Wolsey. In the 1520s he composed three poetic invectives against contemporary abuses in the Church, 'Colin Clout', 'Speak Parrot' and 'Why Come Ye Not to Court' which at first indirectly but with increasing outspokenness reproved Wolsey for his humanist policies and his driving ambition. One main object of attack there is the system of non-residence prevalent in the Church at that time, and for many years to come, whereby a clergyman would accept livings and omit to carry out the duties of the incumbent, living in London far from the parishioners he was supposed to serve. It was the same abuse as Latimer had castigated in his sermon on the absent ploughmen, and a vice of which Wolsey was particularly guilty, amassing from such sinecures the enormous income for those days of £50,000 per year (at a time when even an archbishop earned only £3,000) with which he was able to build Hampton Court. The irony is that Skelton, while composing this vituperative attack was himself permanently resident in Westminster, one hundred miles distant from his Norfolk parish (and the story that he was taking sanctuary there from Wolsey's wrath has long been disproved). At all events, his mordant satires may have been partly responsible for the fact that on Wolsey's fall from power in 1530, Parliament passed legislation against pluralism in livings, though the legislation was largely ineffective.

His adoption of the role of Colin Clout for his attack on the Church was an attempt to resist the more cultivated styles beginning to enter literature. By that device he was able to speak in the guise of a rustic figure, bewildered by the ecclesiastical corruption around him and flagellating it in the language and imagery of an untutored peasant. Skelton could thereby use more naturally the rough unpolished verse to which he had gravitated in his later years, a vigorously native English untouched by the perfumed diction wafting across from Italy and France:

> For though my rhyme be ragged,
> Tattered and jagged,
> Rudely rain-beaten,
> Rusty and moth-eaten,
> If ye take well therewith,
> It hath in it some pith . . .

But there was to be no halting of that continental influence and his rearguard action failed to stem its advance. Such country verse, with its deliberately jerky rhythms and jogging rhymes was to disappear before the refinement of the new poetry. The following stanza by Wyatt was probably written during the very same year as 'Colin Clout', yet stylistically the two are worlds apart:

> When first mine eyes did view and mark
> Thy fair beauty to behold;
> And when my ears listened to hark
> The pleasant words that thou me told,
> I would as then I had been free
> From ears to hear and eyes to see.

The sound is smooth and mellow, the controlled pauses heighten the rhythmic pattern, and the rhyme scheme is more subtly interwoven to create a melodiousness new to English poetry. That melodiousness needs to be seen within a larger context. The love of music had been long established in England. Its composers had been acknowledged as the leaders of Europe until John Dunstable's death in 1453, and even after that, joy in music had continued unabated. Erasmus, as a foreigner visiting the country, had been particularly impressed by the ploughman singing at his furrow and the workman at his bench. Local parish churches were being built from the profits of the booming wool trade (an inscription by one donor, John Barton, reads: 'I thank God and ever shall. / It's the sheep hath paid for all'), and as part of the prosperity organs were now being installed in them to bring church music from the great cathedrals to the smaller communities. But a change in direction occurred during the early decades of the century in response to the new fashions affecting Europe at large.

In music, as opposed to literature, the humanist return to classical sources was by necessity theoretical, for there were no musical scores to be imitated from the ancient period; and even theory, surviving in various philosophical treatises, was very generalised. As a result, music could develop with greater freedom. The Pythagorean concept of universal harmony, with the music of the heavenly spheres intimately related to the harmony in men's souls gave, in its revived form in this century, an enhanced dignity to the arts of song, dance, and musical instrumentation. No longer were they simply pleasant relaxations but were now regarded as a valued conduit for achieving inner concord of spirit, moral integrity, and social acceptability. Castiglione reminded the prospective courtier that '. . . the universe is composed of harmony, the heavens produce music, the human soul is formed on the same principles, and therefore it revives and, as it were, awakens its virtues through music.' An ability to play an instrument and sing from musical notation became prerequisites for the courtier, accomplishments without which he could not participate effectively in social activities, with all their importance for personal advancement. Where paintings and triptychs of an earlier era had depicted the angels playing musical instruments in heaven, now, as in the canvas by Lorenzo Costa (*Plate 6*), interest has turned to human players, achieving a harmony of souls through their unison in part-song. The girl's hand is placed sociably on the lutanist's shoulder, and the positioning of the participants' facial muscles indicates that each singer is producing a different note, blending in musical accord.

England welcomed the vogue from abroad, again as part of a larger educational and moral concept. Henry VIII, who read music at sight and composed his own songs, had by the time of his death assembled one of the finest collections of musical instruments in all Europe, numbering over 380 valuable items; and his own love of dancing he bequeathed to his daughter Elizabeth, whose favourites often included those who were the most accomplished dancers.

The most notable transformation in European music at

this time was a shift away from polyphony (the interweaving of numerous voices, each singing its own specific text, so that the words were generally indistinguishable) to the harmony of one or more voices singing a single text together. In line with Alberti's dictum that an artistic work must consist of the integration of all its parts, the words of the song attained a new prominence. Music was now to correspond closely to the actual words of the text, reflecting each changing mood. Thomas Morley's *A Plain and Easy Introduction to Practical Music* (1597) summarised the principle which had entered English music much earlier in the century, that ' . . . you must in your music be wavering like the wind, sometime wanton, sometime drooping, sometime grave . . . .' The variety now desired by the musician made fresh demands on the poet, and consequently a new expressiveness entered contemporary verse. The lyric particularly and to a lesser extent the sonnet, strove for a generally mellifluous effect but was also modulated internally by the lover's protestations, his sinking into grief, rising into hope, quavering in despair; yet all avoiding dissonance. It may well be that the very division of the sonnet into octet and sestet in this period, with a change of mood at the transition, arose from that tendency towards contrasted emotion within an overall harmony.

Interest in the new modes spread far beyond the court, and the growing demand for songs to be rendered in unison by small groups at all levels of society ensured that the connection between music and poetry was maintained. The most popular poetic miscellany produced during this century, quaintly named *The Paradise of Dainty Devices* (1576), claimed that its poems were '. . . aptly made to be set to any song in five parts, or sung to instrument', and throughout this period even when a poet was not consciously composing for a musical setting, the close inter-relationship of verse and music left its mark upon his writings, contributing to the qualitative difference between Skelton's rougher forms and the harmonious effect of Wyatt's verse.

The Petrarchan sonneteers

Sir Thomas Wyatt (1503—42) was a man of many parts even beyond his distinction as a poet. He was the all-round achiever, excelling in the manifold arts appropriate for the Renaissance courtier. A skilled athlete and swordsman, handsome in appearance, an accomplished linguist and scholar, a know-ledgeable astronomer and musician, he was also held in high regard as a diplomat, both by his own King and by Emperor Charles V. His life had all the makings of splendid success; yet both domestically and politically he had cause for the sadness and sense of missed opportunities which tinge most of his verse. His marriage resulted in an early separation on the discovery of his wife's infidelity. There is strong evidence that he was later Anne Boleyn's lover, compelled to relinquish her with as good a grace as he could muster when it transpired that the rival for her affections was no less than Henry VIII himself. And if his condition was no worse than others in the highly dangerous game of court politics, he was twice imprisoned in the Tower, and on both occasions fortunate to escape with his life. Saved from the executioner's block in 1541, in part by his brilliant defence speech prepared for the trial in which he wittily turned his accuser Bonner into a laughing-stock, he was returned to royal favour. However, in the following year he fell victim to a fever caught while travelling on the King's affairs and died at the early age of thirty-nine.

The melancholy tone pervading his poems may owe some-thing to his personal disappointments, but it derives also in no small part from the love tradition which he introduced into English poetry on his return from a diplomatic mission to Italy in 1527. There the Petrarchan love-poem, fostered and developed for over a century after Petrarch's death, had reached the height of popularity, the tradition in which the despairing lover mourns with icy chills and burning passion the mistress who has denied him her love:

> I find no peace, and all my war is done,
>   I fear and hope, I burn and freeze like ice;
>   I fly above the wind, yet can I not arise . . .

Such verse sounded a new note in England. Its introspective focus upon the emotional state of the speaker, and even its validation of love as an absorbing theme for poetry had little precedence in the English poetic tradition. Earlier poets preferred ballads on the themes of death and ancient battles, or chose narrative, satire, and country scenes for their subject-matter. When they did treat of love, they did so either allegorically or with a lusty forthrightness far removed from the sensitivity of the Petrarchan, as in this anonymous poem of the sixteenth century:

> Western wind, when wilt thou blow,
> The small rain down can blow?
> Christ, if my love were in my arms,
> And I in my bed again!

Now, however, the lover adopts a refined suppliant and mournful tone, pleading for mercy from his cruel mistress, warning the world of the pain inherent in love's bondage and, for all his complaints, obviously revelling in his role as the suffering victim of Cupid's darts. Whether written for a musical setting or not, the following stanza, like most of Wyatt's poems, possesses all the qualities of a text for lute accompaniment. There is the slow plangency of the opening line, the pauses after 'pain' and 'cry' to allow for a more protracted note, soon to be echoed by the rhyming 'I', as the subjective climax of the passage:

> Lament my loss, my labour, and my pain,
>   All ye that hear my woeful plaint and cry;
> If ever man might once your heart constrain
>   To pity words of right, it should be I,
> That since the time that youth in me did reign
>   My pleasant years to bondage did apply,
> Which as it was I purpose to declare,
> Whereby my friends hereafter may beware.

Wyatt wrote a number of poems in this style which for all their intrinsic merit as individual poems and their real contribution to the development of English poetry, when read together lose much of their attractiveness by the repetition of theme and the recurrence of stock images imported with that tradition from abroad. Fortunately, they do not represent his best or his most typical work. Indeed, his modification of the Petrarchan pose, which constituted his finest writing, did much to damage his reputation during the period when that other tradition was in vogue, and even in later years when it was assumed that his main purpose had been only to imitate his fourteenth-century Italian master. He was accused of failing to capture the inward significance of Petrarch's poetry, as if that had been his aim. But Wyatt, we should recall, was writing nearly two hundred years after Petrarch, for a different age and with a different intent, using that tradition for his own ends. In Petrarch's *Canzoniere* the tender longing for an idealised Laura had functioned as a symbol of unfulfilled desire, a yearning for the impossible, representing for the poet an image of life itself, the joy and anguish of man's earthly longing for the divine. There was, for example, no radical change in his poetry after Laura's death from plague in 1348, and her angelic figure is only transposed a little further heavenward.

While Wyatt does adopt the Petrarchan elevation of love as an all-consuming power inspiring man to lifelong dedication or reducing him to abject despair, he combines with that ennoblement the Renaissance penchant for clear, objective perception of fact. At the very moment that he bewails his lot and participates emotionally in the sublime-love tradition, part of him sees with cool cynicism the fickleness of the woman who has caused his agony; and in manly refusal to be imposed upon, he rejects the role assigned to him by the tradition. The Petrarchan mode is thus authenticated and the lover's pain felt by the reader through the speaker's overt rejection of it. But by being viewed here with a certain detachment and even mild humour, the clichés of the tradition are avoided, and the poem achieves a vitality and freshness of its own:

> Divers doth use as I have heard and know,
>   When that to change their ladies do begin,
>   To mourn and wail, and never for to lin,*   *cease
> Hoping thereby to appease their painful woe.
> And some there be, that when it chanceth so
>   That women change and hate where love hath been,
>   They call them false, and think with words to win
> The hearts of them which otherwhere doth grow.
> But as for me, though that by chance indeed
>   Change hath outworn the favour that I had,
>   I will not wail, lament, nor yet be sad;
> Nor call her false, that falsely did me feed;
>   But let it pass and think it is of kind,
>   That often change doth please a woman's mind.

The more virile independence of the lover in such poems may also owe its source to a basic English dislike of 'unmanly' tears. With all their readiness to adopt the imported fashion for the greater sophistication it afforded in the articulation of emotional experience, temperamentally the English were uncomfortable with the role of disconsolate weeper bewailing his lot and in fact responded more readily in this century to the Stoic philosophy, with its demand for equanimity in the face of misfortune. As a result, in the poems they did produce within the sonneteering mode, they were usually at their best when they resisted a collapse into self-pity, displaying instead a slightly mocking tone, an awareness, as it were, of the absurd condition of inferiority in which they unexpectedly found themselves as lovers and a desire at the very least to restore their dignity by a witty rejoinder to their disdainful mistresses.

The sonnet form of this poem, appearing with Wyatt for the first time in England, suggests, together with the great popularity it was to achieve during the century, the need felt by poets for a firmer metrical discipline. The intricate rhyme scheme, the fixed pattern of fourteen iambic pentameters with a separation into octet and sestet, and such further refinements as the final epigrammatic couplet (an innovation of Wyatt's inspired by Serafino and adopted into the Shakespearean form of the sonnet) made sterner demands on the poet than the looser stanzaic modes of the earlier tradition; and the challenge it posed created in poetry a sophistication paralleling the effect which Ciceronian rhetoric had produced in Tudor prose.

In poetry, neither Greek nor Latin verse could serve as metrical models (although they did for subject-matter and genre), since they depended upon a quantitative, non-accentual metre unsuited to English as a non-inflected language. Even the incorporation of continental verse-forms into English required considerable ingenuity on the part of the poet, particularly as the language was still fluid. Spelling (modernised throughout this volume for the convenience of the reader) was, as has been noted, very different at that period, and to a large extent dependent on the passing whim of the writer. Wyatt, like Shakespeare, had various ways of spelling even his own name (Wyat, Wiat) and chose whichever happened to suit his fancy at the time. Such flexibility in spelling has implications both for rhyme and accent. In their original form, the opening lines of the above sonnet read:

> Dyvers dothe vse as I have hard and kno,
> When that to chaunge ther ladies do beginne,
> To morne and waile, and neuer for to lynne,
> Hoping therbye to pease ther painefull woo.

The rhyming of 'know' and 'woe' is seen to have been more dubious at the time the poem was written, particularly as the regional dialects prevailing at the time make it difficult to determine today how the words were actually pronounced. 'Painefull' seems here to contain only two syllables, but there are other times when 'kindely' or 'frendes' (friends) may well have sounded the now silent *e*, adding an extra syllable to the line. Are we always to read such words in the manner that produces the most regular metrical form, or are we to assume that sometimes Wyatt is deliberately varying the metre? When his poems were published in 1557, some thirty years after they were first circulated in manuscript and when Wyatt was no longer alive to supervise the printing, the publisher introduced a number of emendations, either to make words conform to a usage already becoming uniform by then or to regularise the line metrically; but the changes, it can now be seen, generally damage the subtler rhythms of the original, and insofar as it is possible to reconstruct the pronunciation at the time of their composition, they show Wyatt to have been a more sensitive metrist than his publisher had recognised.

The introduction of a final couplet in the sonnet to summarise the theme or sharpen its concluding point indicates the more logical structure of Wyatt's poems, the injection of a more formal reasoning to modify the yearning other-worldliness of the Petrarchan mode. It forms part of a sharper awareness of reality, and there is often in his poems a lively sense of astonishment, almost of rebellion, when he observes, as though standing outside himself, the change wrought in him by love:

> What meaneth this? When I lie alone
> I toss, I turn, I sigh, I groan;
> My bed me seems as hard as stone.
> What meaneth this?

> I sigh, I 'plain continually;
> The clothes that on my bed do lie
> Always methinks they lie awry:
> What meaneth this?

Despite the sharp queries, the melodiousness of the poem is maintained by each stanza's being rounded off with a refrain, again evocative of lute accompaniment. In fact, sonnets constituted only a small percentage of Wyatt's poetry, and he was a keen experimenter in a variety of stanzaic forms. Like the above lyric, they continue, though with a marked refinement in technique and theme, the 'ballet' or 'ballade' tradition of a song to accompany dances which was popular in the previous century. In the following instance, the more complex metrical form of the stanza is used subtly to underscore the theme. As the lines progressively expand in length, the final line is cut short, the sudden ending of each phase marking the unpredictability of the mistress's moods:

> Is it possible
> That so high debate,
> So sharp, so sore, and of such rate,
> Should end so soon and was begun so late?
> Is it possible?
>
> Is it possible
> So cruel intent,
> So hasty heat and so soon spent,
> From love to hate, and thence for to relent?
> Is it possible?

The speaker's incipient rebellion against the role of the suffering lover breaks out at times into open revolt, and the joy of throwing off the yoke and laughing it to scorn comes as a refreshing release from the oppressive self-pity of the older tradition:

> Tangled I was in love's snare
> Oppressed with pain, torment with care,
> Of grief right sure, of joy full bare,
> Clean in despair by cruelty;
> But, ha, ha, ha, full well is me,
> For I am now at liberty . . .

A particularly endearing feature of Wyatt's poems is his habit of addressing a poem not only to his mistress but also to his pen, his heart, his mistress's fair hand in which his own heart is held, and his lute. In each instance, the message of the poem is still aimed at the mistress herself who is assumed to be listening, but the device of addressing her indirectly frees the speaker, as it were, from embarrassment, and creates a greater sense of frankness and intimacy. One of the loveliest of his lyrics is an extension of this device, in which his lute having become the object of her wrath, is defended by him on the grounds that it can only play the songs emanating from its master's heart. If she wishes to change them, then she must, he suggests, change her feelings towards their author:

> Blame not my lute, for he must sound
>   Of this or that as liketh me;
> For lack of wit the lute is bound
>   To give such tunes as pleaseth me,
> Though my songs be somewhat strange,
> And speak such words as touch thy change,
>   Blame not my lute . . .

Within the history of English poetry, Wyatt is a seminal figure. Anthologies have generally restricted him to only one or two poems, such as his deservedly famed 'They flee from me . . . ', with its extraordinarily vivid depiction of a memory from earlier and happier days:

> Thanked be fortune it hath been otherwise
>   Twenty times better; but once in special
> In thin array, after a pleasant guise,
>   When her loose gown from her shoulder did fall,
>   And she caught me in her arms long and small;*   *slim
> Therewithal sweetly did me kiss,
> And softly said, 'Dear heart, how like you this?'

Yet the qualities which distinguish this poem, the mingling of sharply etched actuality with dream-like meditation, of idealised love with scorn for the changeability of women, of melodious tone broken by direct colloquialism, hold true for a large body of his poems which deserve to be classed among the finest of his era. In addition to their own merit, they

were also the first to introduce into the language a new style
of verse in subject-matter, imagery, and metrical form. They
left their mark on English poetry for the following century,
including John Donne among the many heirs, not least in the
latter's use of a fully realised dramatic situation to question
the very Petrarchan convention which acts as its frame.
Nobody previous to Wyatt could have written such lines as:

> A face that should content me wondrous well
> Should not be fair but lovely to behold . . .

but there would be many afterwards who would try to imitate
them.

Poetic miscellanies

By the reign of Henry VIII enterprising printers had begun to
search for new markets, and as a result the poetic anthology
(or 'miscellany' as it was then called) came into being, moulding the tastes of readers during the century, and serving in
later generations as a valuable source for poems which might
otherwise have been lost in manuscript. Although it has only
survived in tattered form (some discarded pages were
discovered within the binding of a later sixteenth-century
volume), the earliest known miscellany is *The Court of Venus*,
probably printed in the 1530s, and containing together with
other poems by various hands some of Wyatt's early lyrics.
The fanciful name chosen for this collection of love poems
was mild compared with the riot of imaginative titles under
which subsequent miscellanies were offered for sale. There
was *The Paradise of Dainty Devices* (1576) which went into
ten editions, *A Gorgeous Gallery of Gallant Inventions* (1578)
orginally named *A Handful of Hidden Secrets* or *Delicate
Dainties, A Handful of Pleasant Delights* (1584), *The Bower
of Delights* (1591), and *The Arbor of Amorous Devices* (1597).
The most influential of them, however, had a more sober
name, *Songs and Sonnets Written by the Right Honorable
Lord Henry Howard Late Earl of Surrey and Others*, and
perhaps because of the solemnity of its formal title it became
commonly known as Tottel's *Miscellany* in tribute to its
publisher Richard Tottel, although the original name was not

forgotten. In Shakespeare's *Merry Wives of Windsor*, the diffident lover Slender, incapable of composing his own love songs, declares 'I had rather than forty shillings I had my Book of Songs and Sonnets here.'

Published in 1557, a year before Elizabeth's accession to the throne, it went into nine editions within the brief space of thirty years, an extraordinary sale by the standards of the time. Unlike most modern anthologies which offer selections from already established poets, this provided the first appearance in print not only for Surrey's poems, but also for the main body of Wyatt's verse, as well as for many individual poems by less famous poets of the generation. Moreover, it offered a dazzling variety of metrical forms, some of them quite new to the English tongue. There was a generous sprinkling of sonnets, ottava rima, terza rima, heroic couplets, blank verse, and rime royal, quite apart from a wide selection of stanzaic patterns for the lyric. In an age when poetry-writing was becoming a fashion at court, it offered a broadened range of models, and confirmed that the continental Renaissance had entered the poetry of England. Tottel at times tampered with the poems he printed, attempting to remove irregularities of metre or harshness of sound usually to the detriment of the original, but such liberties were amply recompensed by the impetus this collection gave to the poets of the Elizabethan era, and the change in reading tastes which it helped to inaugurate.

Although Tottel's *Miscellany* contained ninety poems by Wyatt and only forty by Surrey, the title gave pride of place only to Surrey, probably for reasons of political prudence. Only three years before publication, Wyatt's son had been beheaded for leading a rebellion against Queen Mary, who was still on the throne when the book appeared, and Wyatt's family name had sensitive associations. Surrey (1517–47), it is true, had also been executed for treason, but the circumstances were different. He had been arrested with his father, the Duke of Norfolk, on a transparently absurd charge trumped up by their bitter rivals the Seymours in the jockeying for power as Henry VIII lay dying. Even at that time, the death at the age of thirty-one of this attractive young man who had been a champion at court jousts and had distinguished himself on the battlefield aroused the ire of the populace.

Noble birth in the Tudor era was known to be a dubious blessing, offering a glittering pathway strewn with honours yet leading only too often to the scaffold for no better reason than that the person's very existence as heir or relative to a potential rival marked him out for destruction, and Surrey's memory remained unsullied in men's minds. The prominence accorded to him in the *Miscellany* was largely responsible for his being regarded for many years as Wyatt's superior, but the situation has been rectified in our own era. It can now be seen that, although he did much to smooth out the metrical wrinkles of Tudor poetry and to formalise certain aspects of the sonnet, his own poetry lacks the vitality and lyricism of his older friend and poetic mentor.

Surrey was, by all accounts, happy in his marriage (he wrote a touching lament on his enforced separation from his wife during his military duties) and perhaps for that reason his poems, composed in the guise of the Petrarchan lover scorned by a cold unfeeling mistress, emerge as artificial pieces, as conscious literary exercises, offering an excuse for introducing imagery but without the grief or passion which should generate it:

> Give place, ye lovers here before
> That spent your boasts and brags in vain,
> My lady's beauty passeth more
> The best of yours, I dare well sayn,
> Than doth the sun the candlelight,
> Or brightest day the darkest night . . .

On the other hand, if the lover's suffering is only an excuse for composing poetry, Surrey often leads that poetry in a new direction, towards a deeper responsiveness to the beauty of the English countryside. A love of the changing forms of nature had long existed in English poetry, as in the sparkling opening to *The Canterbury Tales*, but here it merges with the introspective melancholy of the lover to create an emotional bond between speaker and natural scene which has no precedence in English poetry, and was to prove fruitful for its future development. The mythologising of nature familiar from Petrarch's verse is deserted here in favour of the actual world of nature, the nightingale displaying its new feathers in the spring, the adder casting off its winter garb,

the swallow swooping after small flies. In his finest sonnet,
the mood is more solemn, the conventional anguish of the
lover being contrasted with the peacefulness of nature; and
the harmony of the verse here is a tribute to the improved
control of sound and rhythm which Surrey has achieved:

> Alas, so all things now do hold their peace,
> Heaven and earth disturbed in nothing;
> The beasts, the air, the birds their song do cease;
> The night's chair the stars about doth bring.
> Calm is the sea, the waves work less and less;
> So am not I, whom love alas doth wring,
> Bringing before my face the great increase
> Of my desires, whereat I weep and sing
> In joy and woe, as in a doubtful ease.
> For my sweet thoughts sometime do pleasure bring,
> But by and by the cause of my disease
> Gives me a pang that inwardly doth sting,
>> When that I think what grief it is again
>> To live and lack the thing should rid my pain.

If only he had composed more often in this strain, his place
in poetry would be secure; but rarely does he achieve such
distinction and most of his poems fall below Wyatt's in
quality. As this poem shows, incidentally, the so-called
Shakespearean sonnet was already gaining ground, and Surrey
did much to popularise what had been only occasional in
Wyatt's writings. Here the form is still less disciplined than it
was later to become. Although the rhyme scheme follows the
pattern of three quatrains followed by a concluding couplet,
the sense movement spills over those divisions and remains
fluid, so that it would be easy for a reader to miss the fact
that it is a sonnet.

Surrey's further contribution was to be far-reaching in its
effect. For his translation of two books from Virgil's *Aeneid*,
he experimented with a new metrical form, attempting to
domesticate into English the non-rhyming metre of the
classical epic. The unrhymed iambic pentameters or 'blank
verse' he introduced proved so attractive in their combination
of regular rhythm with freedom from the restrictiveness of
rhyme that they became the accepted vehicle for Elizabethan
drama. In Surrey's version, the line is often stiff and awkward,
particularly in the narrative sections; but in the speeches set

within the epic it leaps into life, displaying the rhetorical sweep and power which it was to offer the dramatist:

> He answered nought, nor in my vain demands
> Abode, but from the bottom of his breast
> Sighing he said: 'Flee, flee, O goddess's son,
> And save thee from the fury of the flame.
> Our enemies now are masters of the walls,
> And Troy town now falleth from the top . . .'

Much, then, stands to Surrey's credit as a metrist; but one other verse-form he popularised was to spread like a canker through the minor verse of the age. Jestingly called 'poulter's measure' from the poulterer's habit at that time of adding two extra eggs to the dozen for good measure, it consisted of twelve syllables alternating with fourteen, that is, a six-foot iambic followed by a seven-foot. A clumsy form, it created long, unwieldy lines which pull the reader off balance:

> My soul is fraughted full with grief of follies past;
> My restless body doth consume and death approacheth fast.
> Like them whose fatal thread thy hand hath cut in twain,
> Of whom there is no further bruit, which in their graves remain.

The wonder is that it proved so attractive, becoming in the 1570s the most commonly used metre of all. The resulting verse, abounding in the various Elizabethan anthologies, has by now mercifully sunk into a deserved obscurity.

Surrey employed that metre for his metrical version of certain biblical psalms. There had been a long tradition of such psalm versification, not least because the psalter was so obviously poetic in style, imagery, and content, and yet was not set out as poetry even in the Hebrew original. Only in the eighteenth century was Robert Lowth to discover that Hebrew poetry in fact relied on parallelism, a rhythmic echoing of ideas, free from metrical restriction. Until then, however, poets felt drawn to the task of versifying what seemed such excellent poetic material, with the added attraction that its sacred source might vicariously inspire the poetiser too.

The renewed surge of interest in such activity at this time

was prompted by a further reason. Throughout the Middle Ages, the singing of church masses and hymns had been the prerogative of a clergy trained in polyphonic chant at the various abbeys and monasteries. Now with the advent of the Reformation, the Protestant insisted on a more direct communion between the individual worshipper and his God, and he was encouraged to participate actively in the hymn-singing, preferably within a chapel or smaller church. A need was felt, therefore, for simpler hymns which even the untrained voice could sing, hymns making little demand on musical skill, avoiding complicated polyphony and, if possible, consisting of an easily learnt tune repeated verse after verse. For such purposes, the stanzas needed to be brief, readily understandable even for the illiterate, and simple to remember. Various attempts in this direction were made on the continent by Luther, and later under Calvin. In England, after the dissolution of the abbeys and monasteries around 1539, the need became urgent, and one version appeared which swept the field. It held its position of prominence for centuries, however undeserved that prominence may have been on literary grounds. In 1549, a collection of versified psalms produced by Thomas Sternhold and John Hopkins was published which by the mid-nineteenth century had appeared in no less than *six hundred* editions. Occasionally the authors used poulter's measure, but more commonly they employed a variant of ballad metre (a four-line stanza with alternating four-foot and three-foot iambics, really the 'fourteener' broken into two lines) with the difference from ballad metre that all four lines were rhymed *abab* to aid memorising.

Sternhold and Hopkins unfortunately assumed that the divine origin of the psalms was all the poetic inspiration that their versions required. Accordingly, they merely chopped the ideas of the psalm into metrical form, inserting a meaningless 'I say' or 'then' to fill out a short line or to create an easy rhyme, a sure mark of the lazy poetiser. The result is a succession of stanzas such as:

> O happy is that man, I say,
> Whom Jacob's God doth aid,
> And he whose hope doth not decay,
> But on the Lord is stay'd.

However poor their own attempts which are really doggerel and not poetry, their choice of metre did eventually prove itself and become the accepted mould in which later and more distinguished writers, including Isaac Watts and William Cowper, cast such hymns as 'O God our help in ages past' and 'God moves in a mysterious way/His wonders to perform'. In that respect at least, the sixteenth-century versions apparently found the right answer to the needs of the new Church.

In connection with this theme of pious verse, an oddity deserves to be mentioned which never became part of the mainstream of poetry but was to recur in various forms throughout the centuries, the attempt to counter the popularity of the secular love-song by adapting its success to religious ends much in the style of the rock-hymn sessions, held in churches in our own day. In 1565, John Hall, alarmed at the vogue of amatory verse and hoping to turn it to advantage, issued a volume entitled *The Court of Virtue* in obvious contrast to the secular anthology *The Court of Venus* which had appeared in a new edition three years earlier. In place of Wyatt's well-known lament for unrequited love, which appeared there, beginning 'My lute awake! Perform the last/Labour that thou and I shall waste', Hall offers a poem (to be sung to a popular tune), which opens:

> My lute, awake and praise the Lord,
> My heart and hands thereto accord,
> Agreeing as we have begun
> To sing out of God's Holy Word,
> And so proceed till we have done.

His volume, not surprisingly, did little to stem the tide of the secular love-song, but it does at least indicate how the hymns and religious poetry of this time did, as in subsequent periods, keep a wary eye on contemporary fashions in secular verse and song, lest the younger generation be led astray by its literary or musical attractions.

The change from the cruder notes of Skelton's verse in the earlier part of the century to the polished and sensitive lyrics of Wyatt and Surrey suggest that English poetry was breaking out of its medieval chrysalis to warm its wings in the sunlight of a new era. It was not alone. Drama was undergoing a similar metamorphosis and to that we shall now turn.

4

The growth of secular drama

BY the early sixteenth century, the great cycles of mystery plays spanning Christian history from Creation to Doomsday had begun to die a natural death. After their medieval beginnings, emerging before the high altar of the very church which had forbidden all drama, they had in England reached the height of their dramatic power in the revised Wakefield cycle of the fourteenth century. Such plays continued to be performed well into the sixteenth century and occasionally even beyond, but they had ceased to hold a position of centrality in drama or to attract the best creative writers of the age.

The message disseminated by the Church had itself begun to change. Alarmed at the growing attractiveness of the material world with its expanding economy and widening horizons, it had grown more strident in its reminders to man of the Day of Judgement awaiting him beyond the grave, and his need here in this earthly existence to prepare for the eternity of his soul. Below the fifteenth-century fresco of *The Holy Trinity* by Masaccio, with its startlingly realistic perspective, appears a skeleton laid out upon a coffin with the chilling caption addressed to the spectator: 'What you are, I once was; what I am, you will become!' Its positioning beneath the sacred scene indicated the direction the spectator was to look for eternal life.

In drama, the celebration of the Corpus Christi pageants climaxing in the Crucifixion and Resurrection of Jesus begins to be replaced by such morality plays as *Everyman* (*c*. 1485), where the focus has been transferred from the holy characters of scripture to man himself, to the *psychomachia* or struggle for his soul, with its message that worldly wealth and power would be of no avail to him in postponing either death or the Day of Judgement:

DEATH: Everyman, it may not be, by no way.
I set nought by gold, silver, nor riches,
Nor by pope, emperor, king, duke, nor princes.

As the decades moved on, dramatists were to gaze with increasing fascination at that very power of kings and princes which is so casually dismissed here; and if the theme of Death the Equaliser remains prominent in the later plays, the dramatist's growing sense of astonishment at the fall of such princes from their impressive heights creates in large part the sense of tragic waste.

The demise of the mystery cycles (their name probably arose from a corruption of the Latin *ministerium*) was hastened in England by the break with Rome. Once Henry VIII had claimed for himself the supremacy of the English Church, we find the town clerk of Chester in 1572 altering the document issued each year to announce the performance of the plays by scoring through the warning there that any disturbers of the performance would be cursed by the Pope. The plays, therefore, were now no longer under the jurisdiction or patronage of the Church as such, but of the monarch (a significant change for the development as well as the censorship of drama in England). In those dangerous times, men were understandably wary of risking their heads by performing plays so obviously Catholic in origin, and there is a noticeable drop in the frequency of performance of the cycles after the formal separation from Rome. In 1538, John Bale composed a new Protestant mystery cycle entitled *God's Promises* to replace the Catholic plays, as well as to rival the growing secular drama. It consisted of seven scenes or playlets in which biblical figures obtained from God a renewal of the Covenant, so central to Protestant belief. Noah, like the other characters appearing there, has a self-reliance and dignity in his plea for mercy to man which breathes the spirit of humanism, and the language too is that of the new era:

NOAH: Lose him not yet, Lord, though he hath deeply swerved.
I know thy mercy is far above his rudeness,
Being infinite, as all other things are in thee.
His folly, therefore, now pardon of thy goodness,
And measure it not beyond thy godly pity.

The structure of the drama is, however, outmoded, still clinging to the medieval pattern of the cycle which was to continue only spasmodically through the century before disappearing altogether. Bale had been pouring new wine into a cracked flask.

Some historians have attributed the end of the mystery cycles in England to their suppression by the Protestants,[8] but there is evidence that they would have disappeared in any case. As part of the growing naturalism of the stage, the mystery cycles had in their later period become less formal and stylised. The main characters remained grave preachers of theological doctrine, but among them appeared some with warmer human qualities, anger, humour, and satiric impishness. The change, however, was not uniform. It seeped into the plays only from below. The characters becoming humanised were, it transpires, only those at the lower end of the holy hierarchy. They were either the villains (and hence fair game for ridicule) or figures non-biblical in origin (hence not really holy). The liveliest figures in the more developed cycles included, therefore, Noah's shrewish wife, who does not appear as a recognised figure in the Bible, the shepherds of the Nativity before their conversion to Christianity and, among the villains, Cain with his cheeky servant Garcio and Herod raging among the Innocents. In the course of time the growth of realism spread up the ladder of sanctity until it began to endanger the solemnity of the holier figures. For painters the humanisation of the donors and spectators in the sacred scenes was no threat, since the artist remained in sole control; but an audience roaring with laughter at the antics of minor figures not always obeying the dramatist's instructions was liable to get out of hand. Juan Luiz Vives, a Spanish humanist resident in England, described the cat-calls and ribaldry which he had witnessed at a performance of a Passion play in the Low Countries in the early sixteenth century:

And by and by this great fighter comes and for fear of a girl denies his Master, all the people laughing at her question and hissing at his denial; and in all these revels and ridiculous stirs, Christ only is serious and severe: to the great guilt, shame, and sin both of the priests that present this and the people that behold it.[9]

As a result the realism advancing up the rungs of sanctity from below caused inversely the gradual disappearance of the sacred characters at the top end of the ladder, in descending order of importance. In biblical plays written during the sixteenth century, the first to disappear from the cast is God himself, who could not co-exist with realistic scenes on the stage. Then Christ ceases to be seen in such plays. By mid-century the entire New Testament loses its eligibility for stage presentation, not through censorship but because the dramatists themselves came to realise its inappropriateness for an increasingly naturalistic stage. Dramatists still interested in biblical themes now moved to the less sacred Old Testament and its Apocrypha, which provided the themes for Thomas Garter's *Godly Susannah* (1568) based on the story of Susannah and the Elders, and George Peele's *The Love of King David and Fair Bethsabe (Bathsheba)* at the end of the century in 1594. The last subject with a biblical flavour available for dramatisation at the turn of the century is drawn from the histories of Flavius Josephus in Lady Elizabeth Carew's *Mariam, the Fair Queen of Jewry* (1613), after which even semi-biblical subjects disappear completely from the English stage for three hundred years, moving instead into the unacted closet drama of Milton's *Samson Agonistes* never intended for stage production, and Byron's *Cain*. From this growing sensitivity to the inappropriateness of dramatising the scriptures on an increasingly naturalistic stage, it may be deduced that the mystery cycles and playlets, though still performed in outlying areas, were in any case doomed to extinction.

Such religious plays did not simply disappear, leaving a vacuum behind. The evolution was more gradual, with the new secular drama preserving many of the more popular elements of the earlier plays out of which it had grown. To an Elizabethan audience, Shylock and his servant Launcelot Gobbo would have been immediately recognisable as sixteenth-century versions of the Devil and his comic Vice, particularly as Shylock in that era always wore the red wig and beard familiar from his prototype Judas in the mystery plays. Shakespeare's comic presentation of Vice in Gobbo and Falstaff was itself an outgrowth of those earlier plays. The minor devils of the mystery cycles, running among the members of the audience amidst shrieks of laughter and pretended terror as they laid about them with inflated bladders, had formed an integral part of the festive spirit of those plays, mingling solemnity with comedy; and the moralities had continued that tradition with their humorously leering Envy and supercilious Pride.

The mystery plays had become deeply rooted in the folk-lore of the people, and as late as 1575 the Mayor of Chester, when called before the Privy Council for having permitted the plays to be acted in his city against the regulations, defended himself by insisting, no doubt truthfully, that the people had demanded them. In creating the figure of Shylock, therefore, Shakespeare was relying on a devil tradition still very much alive in people's minds. Moreover, those early plays left their mark on subsequent drama in many other ways, prominent among them being the lavish spectacle which audiences had come to associate with the stage. The theory that pageants were presented from primitive waggons has been considerably modified by recent research. Where they did still move from station to station, it is now believed that, after stopping, the waggons were unloaded and settings used to employ a larger acting area. In later years, the plays were often presented in a fixed setting, and then the invest-ment in time and money was considerable. Indeed, the trade guilds which, as semi-religious institutions, had taken over from the Church the responsibility for the presentation of the plays, were now no longer able to bear the financial burden for individual pageants as in the past, but began to amalgamate in order to share the heavy costs. We know from records that dressmakers and carpenters were hired sometimes four months in advance to prepare the show. In consequence, when the professional stage took over, it was playing to audiences who had come to expect gorgeous robes and colourful processions, and the entertainments and masques in the houses of noblemen had a high standard of spectacle to equal.[10]

The actor's status

The growth of the secular drama in this era was inhibited by the peculiar status of the actor, who was at that time neither a recognised craftsman nor a professional. He had no guild to regulate his activities nor, even more necessary, to offer him the protection he required. The economic difficulties of the country had created problems of wide unemployment and poverty. The most obvious course for a destitute peasant was to wander through the countryside raiding hen-coops and orchards as he went. To contain this danger, which was a threat to all settled husbandry, Poor Laws were passed and strictly enforced, restricting such unemployed vagrants to their town of residence, where the authorities were made responsible for providing them with work or alms. Vagabonds who continued to wander were clapped in irons, 'grievously whipped and burnt through the gristle of the right ear with a hot iron of the compass of an inch about.' The simplest loophole was for such a vagrant to slip a jester's cap into his pocket and, if challenged, to claim that he was an itinerant actor. The loophole was closed in 1572. From that time, only groups of players possessing a document testifying to the personal protection of a nobleman were permitted to tour. Hence the nomenclature for the various actors' companies in this era, such as the Earl of Leicester's Players, or the Admiral's Men. The need for such protection also testifies to the low social status of the professional actor who was at that time rated close to the vagrant, and only towards the end of the century began to rise in public estimation. Hamlet's admonition to Polonius to see the players well bestowed because they are 'the abstract and brief chronicles of the time' was Shakespeare's own hint to the courtiers watching the performance that the actors enjoyed an enhanced social position in his day, and that therefore greater respect should be accorded to them.

In the earlier part of the century, the distinction between amateur and professional actor was less clearly defined. While the mystery plays were still performed mainly by amateurs, plays offered in noblemen's houses began to include in their casts players employed on the staff for that purpose. Moreover, having performed in the house, they would often be permitted to take the play out to the local public, acting at an inn, village green, or hall, so that there were times when an actor himself would be hard-put to define whether his own standing was that of an amateur or a professional.

Interludes

The dramatic form which contributed to the transition from
religious to secular themes as well as from amateur to professional status was the Interlude. The origin of the Latin term
inter-ludum may be a 'play between' the courses at a banquet,
or more simply a 'play between' two or more actors; but
whatever the source of the term, it generally did take place in
the banquet hall during or after a meal. A particularly valuable
contribution of the interlude was its break with the fixed
festival days of the Christian calendar, upon which the earlier
plays had always received their public performance. Presented
within a nobleman's house, the interlude could now form
part of any celebration, such as the visit of distinguished
guests or a family wedding. Such occasions were still festive,
and often coincided with the seasonal rites of Christmas,
Twelfth Night, or Easter, so that much of the anthropological
sense of rebirth or release from winter's stress, which modern
critics have seen as a deeper motive force in comedy and
tragedy, remained present. Yet the possibility of performance
outside the prescribed dates, and their overspill into the
public domain after presentation at the manor-house, opened
the way for the professional stage which could eventually
offer regular week-day performances unconnected with
official public holidays.

Even more significant was the opportunity the interlude
offered for a widening of scope. It could still supply morality
themes, but since it no longer needed to justify itself in the
eyes of the Church, the interlude could also present broad
farce with no moral lesson to convey, scenes from English
history, and even political topics of immediate contemporary
relevance. At first sight these various categories may appear
unrelated, but they were bound by an underlying unity. The
medieval mind loved debate. Peter Abelard's twelfth-century
Sic et Non ('For and Against') had offered contrasting views
on theological matters; the universities had used public
disputation as a basic tool of instruction; and a genre of
poetry had arisen in that period called *débat*, in which two
persons argued their case in verse before a third figure who
adjudicated the prize. The morality play itself was a form of
debate arising from that tradition. Man must judge between

the conflicting advice of the good and bad angels, or between the persuasive claims of the personified Virtues and Vices, each eager to win the prize consisting of the adjudicator's eternal soul. With the advent of humanism, debate continued, but its nature had changed. In morality debates, the dice had been heavily loaded in favour of the virtues whose very names predetermined audience response. Wisdom versus Folly, Charity versus Avarice were black-and-white distinctions, oversimplifications which left little room for subtler discrimination or rational discussion. Hence, while the fate of Everyman may have been in doubt, the choice he ought to make was never in question.

In cultivated courts of the late fifteenth and sixteenth centuries such as Urbino a favourite pastime, as we know from Castiglione's colourful description, was a debate ranging over a wide spectrum of subjects, in which ladies and gentlemen alike would participate with wit and learning under the benign patronage of the Duchess or her deputy, whose only 'cruelty' was to threaten forfeits to anyone reluctant to speak when called upon. They would choose a theme such as the nature of love, the advantage of painting over sculpture, or the attributes desirable in the ideal courtier, and participants would be judged by the company both on their learned reasoning and on the humour with which they presented their arguments. The home of John Morton, in which Thomas More served as page, became at the turn of the century an English counterpart to Urbino, a civilised household presided over by a benevolent and scholarly head, involved at the highest level in the religious and political life of his country of which he was to become Archbishop of Canterbury and Lord Chancellor. More's *Utopia*, with its teasing yet serious discussion of ethical, political and religious topics, reflects the debates in that household much as Castiglione's *Courtier* does for Urbino. And it is not fortuitous that the new interlude emerged from Morton's household and the social and family circle of More who had been educated in it. For the interlude was in many ways a translation into dramatic form of the discussions taking place at the banqueting table, and often spiced by witty jest or humorous anecdote to enliven the argument.

Henry Medwall was a chaplain in Morton's house, who had

been known only for a minor morality interlude entitled *Nature* until the discovery in 1919 of his *Fulgens and Lucrece*. The latter won him recognition not only as the author of the first known secular play in English, but also as an original and lively dramatist. The interlude appears to have been performed about Christmas time in 1497 at a banquet honouring the ambassadors of Flanders and Spain during a period of sensitive international negotiation when it was important to create a warm social atmosphere. The play contains all the ingredients of the interlude summarised above. The central plot is a dramatised morality debate on the theme of Idleness versus Studiousness, but removed from so simplistic and allegorised a contrast into the area of humanist discussion, more in the tradition of Cicero's *De Senectute*. Cornelius, a wealthy young nobleman whose aristocratic forebears have served the state well in the past competes for the hand of the fair Lucrece again Gaius, a plebeian of studious, modest, and wise nature. In addition to his aristocratic blood, Cornelius offers her riches, a life of ease and comfort, beautiful clothes, minstrels to dance by when the mood takes her, and hawks for hunting. Gaius, in defence of his low birth, argues that suitors should be judged by their own deeds, not those of their ancestors, and that in place of idleness, he can offer her a life of moderate riches but greater usefulness and satisfaction. Her choice clearly will fall upon Gaius, but the choice is less easy than the straightforward preference of good over evil and, what is more, is transferred from the abstract world of allegory to the actual world of contemporary social modes, even though the setting is supposedly ancient Rome.

A further merit of the interlude lies in the clever inter-weaving of a comic sub-plot which, like so many such scenes in later Elizabethan drama, humorously echoes or parodies the main theme by being transposed to the knock-about setting of the lower classes. Two servants, named simply A and B, are also in competition for the hand of a 'fair' creature, Lucrece's maid, and are commanded by her to undergo the trial of singing, wrestling, and jousting with each other to determine which is more worthy of her choice. After all their efforts, their only reward at the end is a clout on the head for each, as she laughingly informs them that she is already promised to another.

Here too, as so often in the Renaissance, the lofty debate on the ideals by which humanity is to live becomes anchored by the sub-plot in the everyday setting of serving-men and their wenches, who also form part of that humanity. While the mystery plays had gradually permitted slapstick and humour to creep in from below, it never became an integral part of the overall plan. Noah's fisticuffs with his recalcitrant wife or Garcio's cheeky replies to his master Cain are marginal and later additions, rather like the so-called 'babooneries', those lively drawings of monkeys, a rabbit funeral, or a hunting scene which appear with no connection to the text in the margin of a sacred medieval manuscript, such as a collection of Psalms.[11] With parchment too expensive for an artist to purchase, there was nowhere else for him to draw such scenes except as a decoration to the manuscript he was transcribing. Similarly, with no stage existing in the Middle Ages other than the ecclesiastical, the only place for comedy to grow was in the 'margin' of the religious plays. Now, however, the concept changes. There is an intrinsic relationship between the two plot levels, with the farcical version not detracting from the main debate but enriching it, by broadening its relevance and reminding us that man, for all his noble aspirations, does not live in the clouds but on this solid earth.

The staging of this interlude in a banqueting hall during a festive meal is incorporated into the text as a device for creating rapport with the audience. At the opening of the play, A scolds the diners for sitting at table so solemnly, and asks if they are expecting some pretty girl to dance for them:

> A: For God's will,
> What mean you, sirs, to stand so still?
> Have you eaten, and your fill
> And paid nothing therefore?

Half-way through the performance, as the climactic disputation between the main suitors is about to be presented, an interval is announced:

> A: We may not with our long play
> Let* them from their dinner all day.   *keep
> They have not fully dined.